Busting Free!

HeLpiNg Youth DiscOVeR TheiR iDENTiTY iN ChRist

Neil T. Anderson & Dave Park

Larry Keefauver, Editor

Gospel Light

Gospel Light is an evangelical Christian publisher dedicated to serving the local church. We believe God's vision for Gospel Light is to provide church leaders with biblical, user-friendly materials that will help them evangelize, disciple and minister to children, youth and families.

We hope this Gospel Light resource will help you discover biblical truth for your own life and help you minister to youth. God bless you in your work.

For a free catalog of resources from Gospel Light please contact your Christian supplier or call 1-800-4-GOSPEL.

PUBLISHING STAFF
Jean Daly, Editor
Kyle Duncan, Editorial Director
Gary S. Greig, Ph.D., Senior Editor

ISBN #0-8307-1665-3
© 1994 Neil T. Anderson and Dave Park
All rights reserved.
Printed in U.S.A.

CONTENTS

How to Use This Course

Before you begin teaching, there are a few things you need to know about how this course is designed.

Sunday School Class or Bible Study Group

Some of you are teaching a youth Sunday School class at your church. Others of you are leading a less formal, less structured Bible study group, perhaps at home. This course will work in either setting.

Neil T. Anderson's and Dave Park's Books

The youth are not required to buy or read copies of *Stomping Out the Darkness* and *The Bondage Breaker Youth Edition* in order to participate in this course. However, we strongly recommend that you have copies of the two books available to be given to or purchased by the youth. They will get much more out of the course if they are able to read the corresponding chapters in between sessions.

Survey

Before you begin this course, have your youth complete the Pre-study Survey. This will give you a better idea of the spiritual conditions of the young people in your group.

Course Goal

By the end of this course, you and your group will be better equipped to pursue spiritual maturity and claim spiritual freedom in Christ. After an introductory session (Session 1), the first half of the course (Sessions 2-7) focuses on pursuing spiritual growth, and the second half (Sessions 8-13) focuses on claiming spiritual freedom.

How to Make Clean Copies from This Book

You may make copies of portions of this book with a clean conscience if:

- you (or someone in your organization) are the original purchaser;
- you are using the copies you make for a noncommercial purpose (such as teaching or promoting your ministry) within your church or organization;
- you follow the instructions provided in this book.

However, it is ILLEGAL for you to make copies if:

- you are using the material to promote, advertise or sell a product or service other than for ministry fundraising;
- you are using the material in or on a product for sale;
- you or your organization are not the original purchaser of this book.

By following these guidelines you help us keep our products affordable. Thank you,
Gospel Light

PRE-STUDY SURVEY

Age _____   Grade in School _____   Sex: Male   Female

1. What does it mean to be a Christian? _____

    _____

2. Do you consider yourself to be a Christian?   ❏ Yes   ❏ No   ❏ Not sure
3. Do you believe in reincarnation?   ❏ Yes   ❏ No
4. Do you practice meditation (as in TM or yoga)?   ❏ Yes   ❏ No
5. Do you possess psychic powers?   ❏ Yes   ❏ No, and I'm glad I don't   ❏ No, but I'd like to   ❏ I'm not sure

Respond to the following statements as best you can. You may check as many answers to each statement as apply to you.

6. I have experienced some supernatural presence in my room (seen, heard or felt) that scared me.
    ❏ Never   ❏ When I was younger   ❏ Recently   ❏ All the time
7. I struggle with bad thoughts about God (for example: angry, hateful or cursing thoughts).
    ❏ Never   ❏ When I pray or read the Bible   ❏ When in church
8. I have a hard time concentrating and get distracted easily when I pray.
    ❏ All the time   ❏ Frequently   ❏ Once in a while   ❏ Never
9. I have trouble paying attention during sermons and my Bible reading.
    ❏ Never   ❏ Only when I'm tired   ❏ A lot   ❏ Constantly
10. I have heard "voices" in my head or have had persistent nagging thoughts in my mind that made me feel bad.
    ❏ All the time   ❏ Frequently   ❏ Once in a while   ❏ Never
11. I have struggled with really bad thoughts (lust, hurt, anger, etc.) that I just can't seem to get rid of.
    ❏ Never   ❏ Not very often   ❏ Fairly often   ❏ Often
12. I have struggled with thoughts of suicide.   ❏ Never   ❏ Once or twice   ❏ Recently   ❏ Frequently
13. I have attempted to commit suicide.   ❏ Recently   ❏ More than once   ❏ Once   ❏ Never
14. I have had impulsive thoughts to kill someone.   ❏ Never   ❏ Rarely   ❏ Fairly often   ❏ Frequently
15. I think that the Christian life works for others but not for me.
    ❏ All the time   ❏ Pretty often   ❏ Sometimes   ❏ Never
16. I have been involved with the following: (Check those that apply.)
    ❏ Astral projection   ❏ Table lifting
    ❏ Fortune-telling   ❏ Ouija board
    ❏ Tarot cards   ❏ Blood pacts
    ❏ Crystals or pyramids   ❏ Dungeons and Dragons
    ❏ Automatic writing   ❏ Spirit guides
    ❏ Bloody Mary   ❏ Illegal drugs
    ❏ Palm reading

WHO ARE YOU?

KEY VERSES

"So God created man in his own image, in the image of God he created him; male and female he created them." Genesis 1:27

"The Lord God formed the man from the dust of the ground and breathed into his nostrils the breath of life; and the man became a living being." Genesis 2:7

"But you must not eat from the tree of the knowledge of good and evil, for when you eat of it, you will surely die." Genesis 2:17

BIBLICAL BASIS

Genesis 1:27,29-31; 2:7,17; 3:21; Deuteronomy 26:18; 31:6; Psalm 23:1; 91:11; Matthew 6:28-33; John 1:12,13; 3:16; 10:14; 14:27; 15:15,16; Romans 5:8; 1 Corinthians 12:27; Galatians 3:26-29; Ephesians 4:18; Philippians 4:19; 1 Peter 2:9

THE BIG IDEA

God's purpose for creating us in His likeness was for us to have a relationship with Him. The sinful disobedience of Adam and Eve cut us off from that relationship, but in Jesus Christ that relationship is restored.

AIMS OF THIS SESSION

During this session you will guide students to:
- Discover and share who they are physically, emotionally, mentally and spiritually;
- Identify the strengths they have in their identities in Christ;
- Uncover some weaknesses they have without Jesus Christ.

KEY RESOURCES AND PREPARATION

- Neil Anderson's and Dave Park's books *Stomping Out the Darkness* and *The Bondage Breaker Youth Edition*. Review chapter 1 in *Stomping Out the Darkness*.
- Read all of the Scriptures in this session.
- Secure beforehand all the supplies needed for this session: 3x5-inch cards or mirrors and labels, newsprint, felt pens, a chalkboard or flip chart, chalk, pencils, masking tape.
- Make copies of the worksheets for everyone: "The Physical Me" on page 13 (top half), "The Inner Me" on page 13 (bottom half), "What We Inherited" on page 15 and "Jesus Meets My Needs" on page 17.
- Before the session begins, write this on the chalkboard or an overhead transparency:

Significance	**Security/Safety**	**Belonging**
Genesis 1:29,30	Genesis 3:21	Deuteronomy 26:18

John 1:12,13	Psalm 23:1	Deuteronomy 31:6
John 3:16	Psalm 91:11	John 10:14
John 15:15	Matthew 6:28-33	John 15:16
Romans 5:8	John 14:27	1 Corinthians 12:27
1 Peter 2:9	Philippians 4:19	Galatians 3:26-29

- Pray for your group. If you already know the names of those who will be in the group, pray for them daily by name. Put their names in your Bible or a prominent place in your home. One way you might pray for them is, **Lord God, I ask that you would protect and surround** (name) **with your love and that you would keep any and all evil from influencing him (or her). I ask that his (or her) mind would be his (or her) own, a quiet place, so You might direct and lead him (or her) today. In Jesus' name, amen.**
- Be certain to read Ephesians 6:10-18 and put on the whole armor of God, yourself. Find a prayer partner to pray with you for those in your group and for you. It is important that you are spiritually prepared each day and put a strong prayer covering over yourself and this group as you proceed through this study.

GETTING STARTED (10 MINUTES)

As youth enter the room, give each one a copy of "The Physical Me" and a pencil. Ask them to complete it immediately.

After two to three minutes, collect the worksheets from all of the students. Thoroughly mix the worksheets. Read each physical description to the group. After each one, have the group try to guess who it is. When you get to the last three descriptions, first read all three descriptions. Then have the group try to match the three descriptions with the three remaining people.

Now comment: **It's relatively easy to match what we see physically with the physical descriptions, but it may be more difficult to match descriptions about our inner selves with those in our group. Let's try.**

Now distribute copies of "The Inner Me." Give everyone about three minutes to complete their worksheets and pass it back to you.

Collect "The Inner Me" worksheets and shuffle them thoroughly. After each one is read, ask the group to decide which person best fits that description. Write that person's name on the worksheet and go on to the next. After all the descriptions have been read and a name attached to each, ask the group which of the descriptions had been correctly guessed. Your group may have guessed one-third or one-half correctly. Do not worry about trying to match all of the incorrectly matched ones. Instead, briefly discuss:

Was it harder to match the second set of descriptions than matching the physical ones? Why?

Read Genesis 1:27 to the group. Ask, **What do you think it means to be created in the likeness or image of God?**

GETTING FOCUSED (10 MINUTES)

Divide the students into pairs. It's best at this early stage in the study when group members may not know one another very well to try to pair people with those they do not know. If possible, avoid pairing best friends, couples who are dating one another or youth that are more than a year apart in age. Whenever the session plans in the future call for pairs or trios, continually mix up the group so that by the end of this study most of the group has had the opportunity to meet and share with many different persons.

When you have assigned the pairs, tell them to move their chairs so that they can sit facing one another. Then say: **I want the oldest one between the two of you to go first. I will give you one minute to share your life's history. Then we will switch and the other person will have one minute to share his or her life history. Go.**

After everyone has shared, read Genesis 1:31 to the group. Give these instructions: **God saw that His creation of human beings was good. After Adam and Eve sinned in the Garden of Eden, evil became part of who we are as well. Let's focus on the good things that God gave you when He made you. The youngest person in your pairs will go first. Share five good things about the way God made you for which you are thankful. When one person has finished sharing, the other is to share. Go.**

To encourage sharing, you yourself share five good things about God's creation of you before having everyone else share. For example, you might be thankful for the fact that He created you tall to be able to play basketball or reach high shelves. You might be thankful that God gave you a good memory, certain talents and abilities or a good voice for singing or speaking.

After this sharing, give these instructions: **I am going to read a sentence which I want each of you to complete. The oldest can complete it first each time. After I read a sentence, each of you complete it and then, when all have shared, we'll go to the next sentence.**

1. **What I like best about me physically is:**
2. **If I had created me, what I would have changed about me physically is:**
3. **The feeling I like best when I have it is:**
4. **The feeling I like least when I have it is:**
5. **One good mental attitude I have is:**
6. **One mental attitude that God and I need to work on changing is:**
7. **Spiritually, I am closest to God when I:**
8. **One thing spiritually that separates me from God is:**

Getting into the Word (20 Minutes)

Give everyone in the group a copy of "What We Inherited." Divide the students into three groups. Briefly explain the "Original Creation" figure based on the background given on pp. 21-25 in *Stomping Out the Darkness*. Give each group a large worksheet of newsprint and a felt pen. Have one person in each group volunteer to be the recorder who writes everything that the group says. Tell the recorder in one group to write the title "Significance" at the top of their newsprint. Point to the next group and tell the recorder to write at the top of their newsprint "Safety/Security." Have the recorder in the third group title their newsprint "Belonging." Point to the list of Scriptures you have written on the chalkboard under each of the three categories. Give these instructions: **Have everyone in your group look up a different passage and tell the recorder an answer to this question, "How does God give us significance?" Or, another way to ask the question is, "What is God's purpose for us?" If everyone in the group has looked up one passage and time remains, start looking up a second Scripture until all the Scriptures on the list have been read. Or, in the second group, answer the question, "How does God provide for our safety and security?" In the third group, you will answer the question, "In what ways do we as God's people belong to God and one another?" with your Scriptures.**

Give the groups five minutes to look up their Scriptures and record their responses on newsprint. Then ask each recorder to read the list of what they found to the entire group, and then put the newsprint up on a wall so that it may be seen by everyone.

Have everyone remain in their small groups. Tell the youngest one to go first. Ask each person to complete these sentences:

God says that with Christ I am ....

Without Christ, a person is ....

After everyone has shared, list on the chalkboard some of the thoughts the group had about "who a person is" without Jesus Christ in his or her life. Then read Genesis 2:17 to the group. Have them look at the "Effects of the Fall" figure. Say to the group: **When Adam and Eve were separated from God through sin, spiritual death as well as physical death came into their lives. What are some of the symptoms of spiritual death?** Write "spiritual death" on the chalkboard and discuss. **They also experienced lost knowledge of God.** Read Ephesians 4:18. **In what ways do we see an ignorance of God and His ways in our culture?** Write "lost knowledge of God" on the board and discuss. **They also experienced dominant negative emotions like fear, shame and guilt. Let's list as many sinful, negative emotions as we can.** Write "dominant negative emotions" on the board and list all the ones that the group says. **In the garden, Adam and Eve could only make one bad choice. Because of the Fall, we now have too many choices to make. What are some of the choices we have to make as Christians each day?** For example, "to pray or not to pray." Discuss.

GETTING REAL (10 MINUTES)

Give everyone a copy of "Jesus Meets My Needs." Ask everyone to complete this worksheet and then share with their partner:

The most important need that Jesus meets in my life is ....

One need that I want you to pray for in my life is ....

Ask the partners to pray a short sentence prayer for one another. It might be something like: **Heavenly Father, thank You for meeting all our needs. I pray that you would show** (name) **how You will fill this need in Your timing. In Jesus' name, amen.**

Ask the group to fold up their papers and give them to you. Explain that you will not know who completed a specific paper, but you will know how to pray for the group. Leader Note: This is very important. What the group shares on this worksheet is what you will need to pray for daily. It will also give you insight into the spiritual needs and possible bondages, battles and struggles your group is facing.

GETTING ARMED (5 MINUTES)

Give each person in the group a 3x5-inch card or a mirror with a label on the back of it. Give these instructions: **We have learned that Jesus meets our needs for significance, safety, security and belonging. On your card (or the back of the mirror) complete this sentence from what you've learned:**

Jesus says that I am ....

Write as many things Jesus says you are as you have room. Put this card (or mirror) in your pocket, wallet or purse. Carry it with you each day. Make it the first thing you read each morning this week and the last thing you look at before you go to bed each night.

THE PHYSICAL ME

Complete each sentence with a word or phrase about who you are physically.

My eyes are ....

My hair color is ....

My hair is naturally ....

My height is ....

My skin is ....

-------------------------------------- (cut here) --------------------------------------

THE INNER ME

Write a paragraph that describes who you are intellectually, emotionally and spiritually. Do not describe any of your physical attributes or other physical things about your family or where you live. Below is a sample description:

I am a loving person and my friends tell me I'm a good listener. I enjoy math and biology, but I'm not too good in English or history. I have fun with my parents and family. I have accepted Christ. I care about sick people, and I like dogs. I can't stand cats. I am good at most sports. I'm usually trusting of people and positive about the future.

....

....

....

....

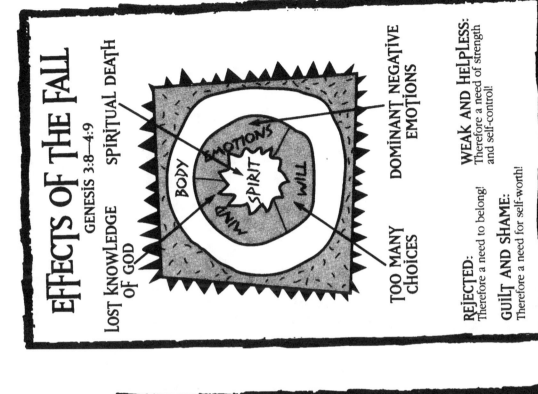

EFFECTS OF THE FALL
GENESIS 3:8—4:9

LOST KNOWLEDGE OF GOD — SPIRITUAL DEATH

DOMINANT NEGATIVE EMOTIONS

TOO MANY CHOICES

REJECTED:
Therefore a need to belong!

GUILT AND SHAME:
Therefore a need for self-worth!

WEAK AND HELPLESS:
Therefore a need of strength and self-control!

(diagram labels: BODY, EMOTIONS, SPIRIT, MIND, WILL)

ORIGINAL CREATION
GENESIS 1,2

PHYSICAL LIFE
United with inner self

SPIRITUAL LIFE
Inner self united with God

SIGNIFICANCE—GENESIS 1:28
Man had a divine purpose.

SAFETY AND SECURITY—GENESIS 1:29f
All of man's needs were provided for.

BELONGING—GENESIS 2:18f
Man had a sense of belonging.

(diagram labels: BODY, EMOTIONS, SPIRIT, MIND, WILL)

JESUS MEETS MY NEEDS

You will not have to share what you write on this paper with your partner. Do not put your name on this paper.

After the fall of Adam and Eve, all of us inherited three basic needs that only Jesus can meet. Are you letting Jesus meet these needs in your life?

Put an *X* where you are right now in your life:

I feel rejected by Jesus and others.	I accept who I am and others accept me.	I know for sure that Jesus loves me.
I feel guilty often.	I sometimes feel guilty.	I know I am forgiven by Jesus, and I feel His forgiveness.
I often think or do shameful things.	I feel shame for past actions or thoughts.	I know and feel Jesus' forgiveness.
I often feel weak and helpless.	I try to live the best I can.	Jesus gives me strength when I'm weak.

What I need from Jesus is: (Check all that you need.)

_____ Acceptance
_____ Ways to cope with family
_____ Forgiveness
_____ Strength to stop doing or thinking shameful things
_____ Power to do what is right
_____ To feel good about myself
_____ Friends who understand me
_____ A way to overcome loneliness
_____ To be stronger in my faith
_____ To grow closer to God
_____ To be loved
_____ Other ....
_____ Other ....

(If you would like your leader to know specifically who you are and to pray for your particular needs, you may put your name on this worksheet. Otherwise, do not put your name on this paper.)

A NEW LIFE AND RELATIONSHIP IN JESUS CHRIST

KEY VERSES

"I tell you the truth, no one can see the kingdom of God unless he is born again." John 3:3

"As in Adam all die, so in Christ all will be made alive." 1 Corinthians 15:22

"Do not let any unwholesome talk come out of your mouths, but only what is helpful for building others up according to their needs, that it may benefit those who listen." Ephesians 4:29

"How great is the love the Father has lavished on us, that we should be called children of God! And that is what we are!" 1 John 3:1

BIBLICAL BASIS

John 3:3; 1 Corinthians 15:22; Ephesians 4:29; 1 John 3:1-3

THE BIG IDEA

My identity as God's child is rooted in what God says about me, not in my appearance, my behavior, others' perceptions of me or Satan's lies about me.

AIMS OF THIS SESSION

During this session you will guide students to:
• Discover who they are in Christ;
• Understand their inheritance from the first Adam and identify what Christ, the second Adam, gives them.

KEY RESOURCES AND PREPARATION

• Read chapters 1-3 of *Stomping Out the Darkness*.
• Read all of the Scriptures listed in this session.
• Secure the following supplies before this session: 3x5-inch cards, pencils, a chalkboard or flip chart, chalk or felt pens.
• Make copies of the worksheets for everyone: "Who Am I?" on pages 23 and 25 and "Since I Am in Christ" on pages 27 and 29.
• Prepare 3x5-inch cards for everyone in your group, writing the titles on them that are listed in "Getting Started."

Getting Started (10 Minutes)

As the youth enter the room hand each one a 3x5-inch card with one of the following phrases written on it: Salt of the earth, Light of the world, Child of God, Part of the True Vine, Christ's friend, Witness for Jesus, Slave of righteousness, Coheir with Christ, New person, Saint, Citizen of heaven, Royal priest.

If there are more people in your group than titles in this list, then repeat some of the names on the 3x5-inch cards. Tell the participants as they enter: **Look at the title on your card. Go around the group and introduce yourself to each person by saying, "Hi, my name is** (name)**. I am a or the** (title on the card)**. Who are you?" For example, I might say, "Hi, I am John. I am a new person. Who are you?" Go around the room until you have introduced yourself to everyone in the room or until I say, "Stop."**

Getting Focused (10 minutes)

Have everyone face the chalkboard or flip chart. Start two columns with one labeled "In Adam" and the other labeled "In Christ."

Then read for the group 1 Corinthians 15:22. Say: **When we were physically born, we naturally inherited certain things from Adam. Let's list some of those things.** Have the students suggest things that we inherited from Adam like sin, death, disease, failure, hard work, pain, suffering, etc. **Now, when we are born again spiritually, we inherit certain things from Jesus Christ.** Read John 3:3 and then list everything that Jesus gives us that reverses what we inherited from Adam. Remind youth that, while they have inherited these things from Christ, they may not always experience these things. You might end up with a list that looks something like this:

In Adam	In Christ
Death	Life
Failure	Success
Disease	Health
Suffering	Joy
Pain	Comfort
Hard Work	Serving God

Now as a whole group discuss these questions:

How did Christ respond to a relationship with God the Father differently than Adam?

If we say that Christ was totally dependent on God, what did Adam desire to be? Some responses might be that Adam desired to be independent, like God, rebellious and disobedient.

What is eternal life? When does it start?

What is the difference between knowing someone and having a personal relationship with someone?

How do you know if you have a personal relationship with Jesus?

Getting into the Word (15 minutes)

Give everyone in the group a copy of "Who Am I?" Divide the students into small groups of three or four persons. Then give these instructions: **Each group will take one section of these truths that the Bible gives to those who trust in Christ.** Assign the groups to the section you wish them to have. **Choose one** truth from that section which you will pantomime for the whole group. **You may not use any words. I will give you about three minutes to plan how you will act out that truth giving everyone else a chance to guess what it is.** Now give the groups about three minutes to decide how they will act out a truth they choose from their list.

After three minutes, give each small group an opportunity to act out for the whole group the truth they have chosen. The whole group must decide with a consensus which truth it is. Then they will see if they have guessed correctly or incorrectly. Have the next small group act out its truth, continuing until every small group has performed. Then return everyone's attention to the worksheet and say: **See how much God loves you.** Read 1 John 3:1-3. **Each one of the things on this list has been given to you by God through Jesus Christ. Beside each truth in your section, note what you know or how you feel about that truth. If there is a truth listed there that you have never heard before, read the Scripture passage listed with that truth. Then, in your small groups, share how you responded to one truth. For example, the first time I saw this list, I realized that I was a saint—not because of how I act but because God says that I am a saint in Jesus Christ.**

When every small group is finished sharing, ask anyone who wishes to share about a truth before the whole group to do so.

GETTING REAL (15 MINUTES)

Give everyone in the group a copy of "Since I Am in Christ." Explain to the group: **When our identity is in Jesus Christ, certain things are true and are a part of our lives. For example, when I am in Christ, sin no longer has control of my life. Look at your list of results from being in Christ. Without reading the Scripture references, let's read the list aloud together in unison.** Read the worksheet in unison. **Now find one other person in the room to be your partner and sit facing that person.** You may need to assign some partners. If someone is left over in the group, you be that person's partner. **Now I want you to reread the list aloud to your partner. Only this time, starting with the oldest person in your pair, read the list to the other person substituting that person's name for the "I" in each sentence. For example, "John is now acceptable to God...." After the first person reads the list to his or her partner, then the second person reads through the list. Go.** After each pair has completed their list, then proceed. **With your partner, share the answers to these questions:** Pause after each question to allow time for brief sharing.

One good change I've noticed in my life is ....

One good thing I wish I would experience more is ....

GETTING ARMED (5 MINUTES)

Read the story about Teddy Stallard from *Stomping Out the Darkness*, pp. 57-59, to the group. Then read Ephesians 4:29 to the group. Say: **Not only do we need to believe God's truth about who we are, we also need to tell others the truth from God about them. Instead of putting them down, we need to build other Christians up through the things we say to them and about them. Right now, tell your** partner the one result from the Lord you see most evident in his or her life and thank God for that result. Say, "I see Christ working in your life through .... Thank You, Lord." Give everyone about two minutes to do this. **Now think of one person who is a Christian that you need to build up and encourage this week. As partners, pray for one another to build up other Christians and yourselves in the Word of God this next week.** After all the pairs have finished praying, form a circle as a whole group. Pray this prayer aloud. **Heavenly Father, reveal to our minds the lies that we believe about ourselves.** Pause. **We accept our new identity in Christ as children of the Most High God and reject the lies that the world and the enemy have taught us.** Pause. **Help us, Lord, to see ourselves as You see us. Change our beliefs so our behavior would change, too.** Pause. **We want to treat others the way that Jesus treated people.** Pause. **In Jesus' name, amen.** Pause.

WHO AM I?

I am the salt of the earth (Matthew 5:13).

I am the light of the world (Matthew 5:14).

I am a child of God (John 1:12).

I am part of the true vine, and Christ's life flows through me (John 15:1,5).

I am Christ's friend (John 15:15).

I am chosen by Christ to bear fruit (John 15:16).

I am Christ's personal witness sent out to tell everybody about Him (Acts 1:8).

I am a slave of righteousness (Romans 6:18).

I am a slave to God, making me holy and giving me eternal life (Romans 6:22).

I am a child of God; I can call Him my Father (Romans 8:14,15; Galatians 3:26; 4:6).

I am a coheir with Christ, inheriting His glory (Romans 8:17).

I am a temple—a dwelling place—for God. His Spirit and His life live in me (1 Corinthians 3:16; 6:19).

I am joined forever to the Lord and am one spirit with Him (1 Corinthians 6:17).

I am a part of Christ's Body (1 Corinthians 12:27).

I am a new person. My past is forgiven and everything is new (2 Corinthians 5:17).

I am at peace with God, and He has given me the work of helping others find peace with Him (2 Corinthians 5:18,19).

I am a child of God and one with others in His family (Galatians 3:26,28).

I am a child of God and will receive the inheritance He has promised (Galatians 4:6,7).

I am a saint, a holy person (Ephesians 1:1; Philippians 1:1; Colossians 1:2).

I am a citizen of heaven seated in heaven right now (Ephesians 2:6; Philippians 3:20).

I am God's building project, His handiwork, created in Christ to do His work (Ephesians 2:10).

I am a citizen of heaven with all of God's family (Ephesians 2:19).

I am a prisoner of Christ so I can help others
(Ephesians 3:1; 4:1).
I am righteous and holy (Ephesians 4:24).
I am hidden with Christ in God (Colossians 3:3).
I am an expression of the life of Christ because He is my life
(Colossians 3:4).
I am chosen of God, holy and dearly loved (Colossians 3:12;
1 Thessalonians 1:4).
I am a child of light and not of darkness (1 Thessalonians 5:5).
I am chosen to share in God's heavenly calling (Hebrews 3:1).
I am part of Christ; I share in His life (Hebrews 3:14).
I am one of God's living stones, being built up in Christ as a spir-
itual house (1 Peter 2:5).
I am a member of a chosen race, a royal priesthood, a holy
nation, a people belonging to God (1 Peter 2:9,10).
I am only a visitor to this world in which I temporarily live
(1 Peter 2:11).
I am an enemy of the devil (1 Peter 5:8).
I am a child of God, and I will be like Christ when He returns
(1 John 3:1,2).
I am born again in Christ, and the evil one—the devil—cannot
touch me (1 John 5:18).
I am *not* the great "I am" (Exodus 3:14; John 8:24,28,58), but by
the grace of God, I am what I am (1 Corinthians 15:10).

SINCE I AM IN CHRIST, BY THE GRACE OF GOD...

I am now acceptable to God (justified) and completely forgiven. I live at peace with Him (Romans 5:1).

The sinful person I used to be died with Christ, and sin no longer rules my life (Romans 6:1-6).

I am free from the punishment (condemnation) my sin deserves (Romans 8:1).

I have been placed into Christ by God's doing (1 Corinthians 1:30).

I have received God's Spirit into my life. I can recognize the blessings He has given me (1 Corinthians 2:12).

I have been given the mind of Christ. He gives me His wisdom to make right choices (1 Corinthians 2:16).

I have been bought with a price; I am not my own; I belong to God (1 Corinthians 6:19,20).

I am God's possession, chosen and secure in Him (sealed). I have been given the Holy Spirit as a promise of my inheritance to come (2 Corinthians 1:21,22; Ephesians 1:13,14).

Since I have died, I no longer live for myself, but for Christ (2 Corinthians 5:14,15).

I have been made acceptable to God (righteous) (2 Corinthians 5:21).

I have been crucified with Christ and it is no longer I who live, but Christ lives in me. The life I now live is Christ's life (Galatians 2:20).

I have been blessed with every spiritual blessing (Ephesians 1:3).

I was chosen in Christ to be holy before the world was created. I am without blame before Him (Ephesians 1:4).

I was chosen by God (predestined) to be adopted as His child (Ephesians 1:5).

I have been bought out of slavery to sin (redeemed) and forgiven. I have received His generous grace (Ephesians 1:7,8).

I have been made spiritually alive just as Christ is alive (Ephesians 2:5).

I have been raised up and seated with Christ in heaven (Ephesians 2:6).

I have direct access to God through the Spirit (Ephesians 2:18).

I may approach God with boldness, freedom and confidence (Ephesians 3:12).

I have been rescued from the dark power of Satan's rule and have been brought into the kingdom of Christ (Colossians 1:13).

I have been forgiven of all my sins and set free. The debt against me has
been cancelled (Colossians 1:14).

Christ Himself lives in me (Colossians 1:27).

I am firmly rooted in Christ and am now being built up in Him
(Colossians 2:7).

I am fully grown (complete) in Christ (Colossians 2:10).

I am spiritually clean. My old sinful self has been removed
(Colossians 2:11).

I have been buried, raised and made alive with Christ (Colossians 2:12,13).

I died with Christ and I have been raised up with Christ. My life is now hidden with Christ in God. Christ is now my life (Colossians 3:1-4).

I have been given a spirit of power, love and self-control (2 Timothy 1:7).

I have been saved and set apart (sanctified) according to God's plan
(2 Timothy 1:9; Titus 3:5).

Because I am set apart (sanctified) and one with Christ, He is not ashamed
to call me His brother or sister (Hebrews 2:11).

I have the right to come boldly before the throne of God. He will meet my
needs lovingly and kindly (Hebrews 4:16).

I have been given great and valuable promises. God's nature has become a
part of me (2 Peter 1:4).

LETTING YOUR NEW NATURE SHINE

KEY VERSES

"When I want to do good, I don't; and when I try not to do wrong, I do it anyway. Oh, what a terrible predicament I'm in!" Romans 7:19,24 (*TLB*)

"Therefore, if anyone is in Christ, he is a new creation; the old has gone, the new has come!" 2 Corinthians 5:17

"As for you, you were dead in your transgressions and sins, in which you used to live when you followed the ways of the world and of the ruler of the kingdom of the air, the spirit who is now at work in those who are disobedient. All of us also lived among them at one time, gratifying the cravings of our sinful nature and following its desires and thoughts. Like the rest, we were by nature objects of wrath." Ephesians 2:1-3

"For you were once darkness, but now you are light in the Lord. Live as children of light." Ephesians 5:8

Also read Romans 8; Galatians 5; 1 Corinthians 2,3.

BIBLICAL BASIS

John 8:32; 10:10; Romans 6:6; 7:19,24; 8; 1 Corinthians 2,3; 2 Corinthians 5:17; Galatians 2:20; 5; Ephesians 2:1-3; 5:8

THE BIG IDEA

Every child of God has the power to live a Spirit-controlled life, confessing sin and bearing the fruit of the Spirit.

AIMS OF THIS SESSION

During this session you will guide students to:

- Learn about how the natural or "old man" is crucified with Christ, and how the Holy Spirit gives power and guidance to body, soul and spirit;
- Understand why a Christian continues to sin after being saved and what to do about sin in one's life;
- Know how to resist the temptations and desires of the flesh while walking in the Spirit and bearing spiritual fruit.

KEY RESOURCES AND PREPARATION

- Read chapters 4 and 5 in *Stomping Out the Darkness*.
- Read all of the Scripture passages in this session.
- Secure all supplies needed for this session: red and gold chenille wires or yarn, pencils, three signs with

string on them to hang around the necks of each person in the role play. Letter "BODY = flesh" on one sign, "SOUL = mind, will, emotions" on another and "SPIRIT" on the third.

- Make copies of "What's Your Nature?" on page 35 and "The Three Lives" on pages 37 and 39 for everyone in your group. Make copies of "Role Plays" on page 41 for the actors.
- Pray for each group participant that their new nature will resist temptation and receive the power of the Holy Spirit to bear fruit.

Getting Started (10 minutes)

As young people enter the session, hand them a copy of "What's Your Nature?" Give them a pencil and instruct them to complete the survey without looking up the Scripture references. Once they have completed the surveys, divide the students into groups of three to four persons. Ask the small groups to check their answers by looking up the Scripture references until everyone has the correct answers. After a few minutes give everyone the answers. (1. False; 2. False; 3. False; 4. True; 5. False; 6. True; 7. True.)

Getting Focused (10 minutes)

Keep everyone in their small groups of three to four persons. Give everyone a red chenille wire. Explain that this represents their sin natures before they became new creations in Jesus Christ. Now give everyone a piece of gold chenille wire. Explain that this wire represents their new natures once Christ is Lord over their lives. Give these instructions: **Discuss in your groups how to represent with your chenille wires what happens when a person becomes a new creation in Jesus. You can do anything with your chenille wires that you choose to represent how a Christian becomes a new creation. You can link, tie, wrap and shape your chenille wires in any shape to represent the old person and the new person in Christ. You have three minutes to mold your sculptures. Pick one person from your group to explain your sculpture to the rest of us.**

After every group has explained their sculptures, you take one red chenille wire and shape it into a person. Do the same with a gold chenille wire. Explain: **This first person shaped from a red chenille wire has a total sin nature. The second person shaped from a gold chenille wire represents the new person in Christ. The old nature is crucified, destroyed, when we are in Christ.** Read Romans 6:6; Galatians 2:20. **However, we still sin. We are not under the power or obligation to sin as Christians. We do so because we willfully violate our new nature in Christ. Such sin must be confessed and turned away from. This is called "repentance."**

Discuss as a whole group the various sculptures and how they did or did not reflect the new and old natures. Explore these questions:

Why do Christians sin?

What do we need to do when we sin?

What does it mean to renounce something?

Why do old, sinful habits keep creeping into our new lives as Christians?

Is it possible for a Christian to resist sin when tempted? How do we resist sin?

GETTING INTO THE WORD (15 MINUTES)

Give each person a copy of "The Three Lives." Take a few minutes to explain each figure, carefully reading each Scripture and describing how a child of God learns to say no to the flesh and yes to the Holy Spirit.

Ask for nine volunteers, three people for each role play. (If your group is small, the same three volunteers can be used in each role play.) Give each volunteer a copy of "Role Plays" and assign a role play to each group. Explain that you will ask them to role-play the body, soul and spirit. Using an overhead projector or chalkboard, draw "The Natural Person" figure.

Ask volunteers to read their role play and determine what their person looks like and does. Answer any questions they have. Have each group role-play their script in front of the rest of the group using the signs you have prepared.

After the role plays, discuss:

What happens when we simply live in the flesh and are unsaved?

In Role Play Two, what was in control? How did that control affect the Soul and the Body?

How was Role Play Three different from Role Play Two? How do we grieve and resist the Spirit as Christians?

GETTING REAL (10 MINUTES)

Read Galatians 5:16-18 to the group. Explain: **When we walk in the Spirit, our lives will bear the fruit of the Spirit. We are free from artificial rules and legalism. The Holy Spirit wants to live through us. Let's read Galatians 5:22 and see how the Spirit lives through us. Get with one other person.**

Share with each other, which of the fruit really shines through your lives and which has difficulty shining through.

Share one area of your life in which you resist the leading of the Holy Spirit.

GETTING ARMED (5 MINUTES)

Explain: **In Proverbs 28:13, God's Word asks us to confess and renounce our sin. Confession is agreeing with God that you have sinned. Renunciation means to repent or turn your back on your sinful ways. Only when we confess and renounce our sin are we able to walk in the Spirit.** Ask everyone to pray in silence as you lead this guided prayer. **Confess to the Lord one area of your life that you really resist the Spirit in the flesh.** Pause. **Ask the Lord to forgive you.** Pause. **Renounce that sin.** Pause. **Thank the Lord for one fruit of the Spirit you see in your life.** Pause. **Pray after me...Holy Spirit...lead my life...direct my mind to thoughts only of You...help me to resist temptation...crucify my flesh...in Jesus' name, amen.**

WHAT'S YOUR NATURE?

What kind of nature does a Christian have according to the Bible? Write *T* for true or *F* for false before each statement.

_____ 1.   We are part saints and part sinners (see 2 Corinthians 5:17).

_____ 2.   Saints never sin (see Romans 7:19,24).

_____ 3.   Within Christians, the old and new natures are constantly at war with one another (see 2 Corinthians 5:17).

_____ 4.   Once, as unbelievers, we were in the kingdom of darkness, but now as believers, we are in the kingdom of light (see Romans 8:9).

_____ 5.   Christians are sinners saved by grace and hanging on until the rapture (see Romans 8:35-38).

_____ 6.   When a Christian accepts the truth that he or she is a new creature on the inside, then that Christian will start living successfully and victoriously (see John 8:32; 10:10).

_____ 7.   Before a person becomes a Christian, that person is God's enemy and by nature a child of wrath (see Ephesians 2:1-3).

THE NATURAL PERSON
Life "In the Flesh"
1 Corinthians 2:14

FLESH (Romans 8:8)
Though flesh can mean the body, it is the learned independence which gives sin its opportunity. The natural man who tries to find purpose and meaning in life independently of God is going to struggle with inferiority, insecurity, inadequacy, guilt, worry, and doubts.

BODY
Tension or migraine headaches, nervous stomach, hives, skin rashes, allergies, asthma, some arthritis, spastic colon, heart palpitations, respiratory ailments, etc.

EMOTIONS
Bitterness, anxiety, depression, etc.

SPIRIT
Man's spirit is dead to God (Ephesians 2:1-3); thus, the natural man is unable to fulfill the purpose for which he was created. Lacking life from God, sin is inevitable.

MIND
Obsessive thoughts, fantasy, etc.

WILL (Galatians 5:16-18)
Walk after the flesh
immorality
impurity
lustfulness
idolatry
witchcraft
hatred
strife
outbursts
of anger
jealousy
disputes
dissensions
factions
envying
drunkenness
carousing

THE SPIRITUAL PERSON
Life "In the Spirit"
1 Corinthians 2:15

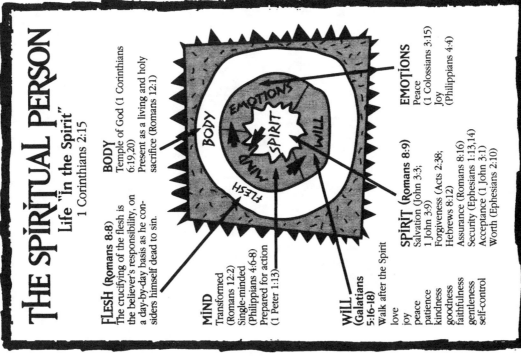

FLESH (Romans 8:8)
The crucifying of the flesh is the believer's responsibility, on a day-by-day basis as he considers himself dead to sin.

BODY
Temple of God (1 Corinthians 6:19,20)
Present as a living and holy sacrifice (Romans 12:1)

MIND
Transformed (Romans 12:2)
Single-minded (Philippians 4:6-8)
Prepared for action (1 Peter 1:13)

WILL (Galatians 5:16-18)
Walk after the Spirit
love
joy
peace
patience
kindness
goodness
faithfulness
gentleness
self-control

SPIRIT (Romans 8:9)
Salvation (John 3:3;
1 John 3:9)
Forgiveness (Acts 2:38;
Hebrews 8:12)
Assurance (Romans 8:16)
Security (Ephesians 1:13,14)
Acceptance (1 John 3:1)
Worth (Ephesians 2:10)

EMOTIONS
Peace
(1 Colossians 3:15)
Joy
(Philippians 4:4)

THE FLESHLY PERSON
Life "According to the Flesh"
1 Corinthians 3:3

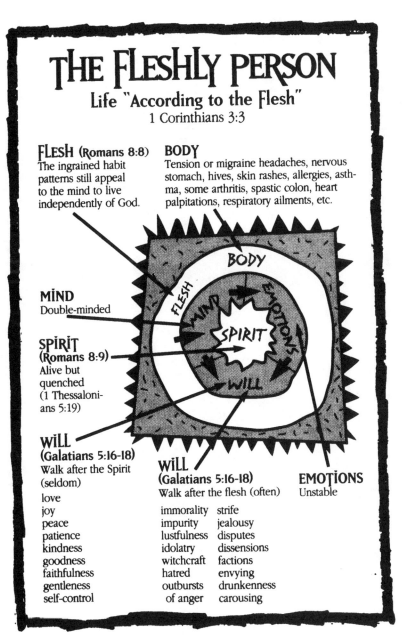

FLESH (Romans 8:8)
The ingrained habit patterns still appeal to the mind to live independently of God.

BODY
Tension or migraine headaches, nervous stomach, hives, skin rashes, allergies, asthma, some arthritis, spastic colon, heart palpitations, respiratory ailments, etc.

MIND
Double-minded

SPIRIT (Romans 8:9)
Alive but quenched (1 Thessalonians 5:19)

WILL (Galatians 5:16-18)
Walk after the Spirit (seldom)

love
joy
peace
patience
kindness
goodness
faithfulness
gentleness
self-control

WILL (Galatians 5:16-18)
Walk after the flesh (often)

immorality   strife
impurity   jealousy
lustfulness   disputes
idolatry   dissensions
witchcraft   factions
hatred   envying
outbursts   drunkenness
  of anger   carousing

EMOTIONS
Unstable

ROLE PLAYS

Role Play One

This person is spiritually dead, separated from God, living independently from God. He has a soul, meaning he can think, feel and choose, but his mind, emotions and will are directed by his flesh, which acts completely apart from the God who created him. The natural person may think he is free to choose his behavior. But since he lives in the flesh, he can't help but walk *according* to the flesh. The natural person also has a body, of course, but he has no spiritual resources for coping with the stresses of life or making positive choices. So he may fall victim to one or more of the physical problems.

Role Play Two

This person has been remarkably transformed from the natural person he was before spiritual birth. When he accepted Christ, his spirit was united with God's Spirit. He now receives his power from the Spirit, not from the flesh. His mind has been totally changed and made new. His emotions are marked by peace and joy instead of turmoil. And he is free to choose *not* to walk according to the flesh, but to walk according to the Spirit. The body of the spiritual person is now a place where the Holy Spirit lives. The spiritual person offers his body as a living sacrifice of worship and service to God. The flesh, which was trained to live without God under the old self, is still there in the spiritual person. But he obediently puts to death the flesh and its desires daily.

Role Play Three

The fleshly person is a Christian, spiritually alive in Christ and declared righteous by God. But instead of being directed and controlled by the Spirit, this believer chooses to follow the temptations of his flesh. As a result, his mind is full of sinful thoughts and he has a lot of negative emotions. And, although he is free to walk in the Spirit and produce fruit, he chooses to get involved in sinful activity by doing what his flesh suggests. His physical body is a temple of God in bad shape.

POSITIVE FAITH PRODUCES TRUE HAPPINESS AND A CHRISTLIKE CHARACTER

KEY VERSES

"Be strong and very courageous. Be careful to obey all the law my servant Moses gave you; do not turn from it to the right or to the left, that you may be successful wherever you go. Do not let this Book of the Law depart from your mouth; meditate on it day and night, so that you may be careful to do everything written in it. Then you will be prosperous and successful." Joshua 1:7,8

"Not only so, but we also rejoice in our sufferings, because we know that suffering produces perseverance; perseverance, character; and character, hope. And hope does not disappoint us, because God has poured out his love into our hearts by the Holy Spirit, whom he has given us." Romans 5:3-5

"We live by faith, not by sight." 2 Corinthians 5:7

"His divine power has given us everything we need for life and godliness through our knowledge of him who called us by his own glory and goodness. Through these he has given us his very great and precious promises, so that through them you may participate in the divine nature and escape the corruption in the world caused by evil desires. For this very reason, make every effort to add to your faith goodness; and to goodness, knowledge; and to knowledge, self-control; and to self-control, perseverance; and to perseverance, godliness; and to godliness, brotherly kindness; and to brotherly kindness, love. For if you possess these qualities in increasing measure, they will keep you from being ineffective and unproductive in your knowledge of our Lord Jesus Christ. But if anyone does not have them, he is nearsighted and blind, and has forgotten that he has been cleansed from his past sins. Therefore, my brothers, be all the more eager to make your calling and election sure. For if you do these things, you will never fall." 2 Peter 1:3-10

"Now faith is being sure of what we hope for and certain of what we do not see. By faith we understand that the universe was formed at God's command, so that what is seen was not made out of what was visible." Hebrews 11:1,3

BIBLICAL BASIS

Joshua 1:7,8; Romans 5:3-5; 2 Corinthians 5:7; Philippians 4:4,6,7; 1 Timothy 4:7,8; 6:8; 2 Timothy 4:7; Hebrews 11:1,3; 12:1-3; 1 Peter 4:10; 2 Peter 1:3-10

THE BIG IDEA

God's plan and goals for your life focus on developing a Christlike character in you as lived out through your daily walk with God in your beliefs, feelings and actions.

AIMS OF THIS SESSION

During this session you will guide students to:
- Learn what God's plan is for their lives and how their own personal goals and plans need to conform to God's;
- Explore the Christlike character God is forming in each of their lives;
- Evaluate where they are personally in their walk of faith.

KEY RESOURCES AND PREPARATION

- Read chapters 6-8 of *Stomping Out the Darkness*.
- Read all the Scriptures mentioned in this session.
- Do the worksheets yourself. Be willing to share how you answered some of the evaluations so as to model for the group the need for sharing openly and honestly.
- Pray for God's plan and goals in each person's life in your group. Pull down the strongholds and pray against anxiety, depression and anger in the lives of your group members.
- Make copies of the worksheets for everyone in the group: "What Do You Trust?" on page 47 and "God's Guidelines for My Walk of Faith" on page 49.
- Have a videocassette recording of *Indiana Jones and the Last Crusade*, a VCR and monitor, pencils, extra Bibles, a chalkboard or flip chart, chalk or felt pens.
- Be completely familiar with the situations you will ask the group to mime through role-playing.

GETTING STARTED (10 MINUTES)

As soon as the group has arrived, show the film segment from *Indiana Jones and the Last Crusade* described in *Stomping Out the Darkness*, chapter 6, p. 96. For those who haven't seen the film, give a brief description of the film's plot. Most of your group will have seen the film.

If you do not wish to show the video clip, then have one person in the group volunteer to "take a risk." Blindfold that person saying that you will verbally direct him or her in walking around the room so that they will not walk into anyone or anything in the room. Assign someone to take the blindfolded person out of the room so that they cannot hear what you tell the rest of the group. When they are out of earshot, tell the rest of the group to make all kinds of noises and give false directions while you are giving true directions. Bring the blindfolded person back in and start the exercise. After you have given directions to that person for walking around the room blindfolded for about a minute, stop the exercise and discuss:

Did Indiana Jones or the blindfolded person really know where to go without help?

How do we know where to go with our lives without faith?

Read Hebrews 11:1,3 and 2 Corinthians 5:7. If we cannot see God, how can we learn to trust Him?

GETTING FOCUSED (10 MINUTES)

Divide the students into pairs and give each pair copies of "What Do You Trust?" Give the pairs two minutes to complete the survey and then say: **Share with your partner two or three of those things on the list**

you trust the most and those you trust the least. Pause about two minutes. **Now as a group let's see which ones we trust the most.**

Poll the group by reviewing the items, and list on the chalkboard how many checked "absolutely" by each item. Then poll and list the items that were most often checked as "none." Discuss the reasons that the group has as to why people trusted certain items so strongly and why other things were not trusted much at all.

GETTING INTO THE WORD (20 MINUTES)

Say to the group: **Faith is an action word.** Point to someone in the group. Ask them if they are willing to fall backwards and let you catch them. When they say "yes," then ask them to come to the front of the group and fall backwards while you catch them. **You see, faith is not saying you will fall, but actually doing it. Being willing to fall also depends on the trust you have in the person catching you. Since God can be absolutely trusted in faith, if we stumble in our faith walk, will God catch us? Does God love us just the way we are in the midst of our weaknesses, failures and sin? Is there anything we can do to make God stop loving us? In fact, will God ever love us more or less than He loves us right now?** Take time to discuss these questions. **Sometimes our feelings tell us just how much we are trusting God in faith at that moment. If we are angry, depressed, feeling defeated or anxious, we may not be really believing that God can or will help us with our plans and problems. We may be setting plans and goals for our lives that are not in harmony with God's plans or basing our happiness on an unhealthy, unrealistic, hopeless goal that we have set for our lives.**

Discuss with your partner an unrealistic goal you set for yourself that, when you didn't make it, you became depressed, angry or anxious. Also share a realistic goal that God helped you set and accomplish. Give two minutes for this sharing. **For example, you may set a goal to be on a team or in a club that requires skills beyond your ability. Then when someone else gets accepted and you do not, you may worry about your self-worth, become depressed or even get angry with someone else who does make the team or get into the club. So, what does the Bible say are good goals? What are the differences between God's goals and ideas for us and our own desires and wants? How can faith in God help us achieve His plan and goals for our lives? God's basic goal for our lives is to become like Christ—that's called character development. Let's explore what Romans 5:3-5 says about how faith in God builds the kind of character He wants in our lives.**

Have everyone read Romans 5:3-5 in the *NIV* translation. Divide the students into three groups. Label the groups:

Group 1: Tribulation brings about perseverance.
Group 2: Perseverance brings about character.
Group 3: Character brings about hope without disappointment.

Each group is to think of a situation at home, church or school that would illustrate this point. For example, a sophomore might have to suffer through a junior varsity season in order to learn how to wait for the time he or she can be on the varsity team. Or, a guy decides to wait on satisfying his sexual drives until marriage and develops a moral character. Or, a student who has developed a truthful character is hoping for a job and gets hired over someone who has lied on a job application.

After each group has thought of a real-life situation that illustrates their theme from Romans 5, they must then role-play the situation in mime, i.e. in silence without spoken dialogue. The rest of the group tries to guess what has happened in the situation and how that illustrates the theme of that group. Take about five minutes for each group to come up with their situation and practice their role play out of sight of the other groups. Then have each group present their role play and discuss after each one:

How does that situation illustrate the text from Romans 5?
What are other situations that might illustrate the theme of that group?

Getting Real (10 Minutes)

Ask everyone in the group to look up 2 Peter 1:3-10. Explain: **This passage lists the qualities God is creating in our character to make us Christlike. Call out the qualities you see in this passage and I will list them on the chalkboard.** Write the title "Qualities" on the chalkboard and make a list under it of the qualities the group finds in the text. **The Bible also tells us how to be successful in growing these qualities in our character. Read Joshua 1:7,8. Now let's list what we must do to grow these qualities of character.** List what the group finds in the text all the things God commands us to do. **With your partner, share this:**

Which quality has grown the most in your life in the last few months? Which one the least?
From the list we made from Joshua, what do you need to do the most to grow in your Christian walk and become more like Jesus?

Give everyone in the group a copy of "God's Guidelines for My Walk of Faith." Ask everyone to read the guidelines and the passages listed, then to complete the self-evaluation. After this, ask them to share with their partners one guideline for which they would like prayer. Give the pairs about five minutes for this.

Getting Armed (5 minutes)

Tell the group: **On the back of your worksheet, write in one or two sentences the kind of character God wants you to have.** Pause. **Now ask yourself, "Do my beliefs and goals line up with God's? Are my feelings positive or negative about God, myself and others? Are my actions disciplined so that God can develop Christ's character in me?"**

Write a prayer that asks God to develop Christ's character in you. Pray that prayer. Now take the prayer with you and reread it and pray it daily this week.

WHAT DO YOU TRUST?

Faith or trust depends on what we believe and in what we trust. What or whom can you really trust? Check where your trust is on each object of the trust list.

I Trust:	Absolutely	Strongly	Somewhat	Rarely	None
Money					
Parents					
Friends					
Church					
School					
President					
Politicians					
Salesmen					
Ministers					
Bible					
Jesus					
Textbooks					
Teachers					
Banks					
Family					
Myself					

God's Guidelines for My Walk of Faith

Read the passage for each guideline. Grade yourself from *A* to *NI* (needs improvement) in each guideline. What area of your walk of faith needs the most prayer and growth?

1. Success comes from accepting and pursuing God's goals for my life. Hebrews 12:1-3. Grade:.................

2. Significance comes from proper use of time. If I want to increase my importance I must do really important things with my time. 1 Timothy 4:7,8. Grade:...................

3. Fulfillment comes from serving others. 1 Peter 4:10. Grade:...................

4. Satisfaction comes from living a quality life and having quality relationships. 2 Timothy 4:7.

   Grade:...................

5. Happiness comes from wanting or being content with what you have. 1 Timothy 6:8. Grade:...............

6. Fun comes from enjoying life moment by moment, seeking only to please God. Philippians 4:4.

   Grade:...................

7. Peace in my heart comes from trusting God even in the tough times. Philippians 4:6,7. Grade:..............

WINNING THE BATTLE FOR YOUR MIND

KEY VERSES

"As the heavens are higher than the earth, so are my ways higher than your ways, and my thoughts than your thoughts." Isaiah 55:9

"For though we live in the world, we do not wage war as the world does. The weapons we fight with are not the weapons of the world. On the contrary, they have divine power to demolish strongholds. We demolish arguments and every pretension that sets itself up against the knowledge of God, and we take captive every thought to make it obedient to Christ." 2 Corinthians 10:3-5

"Finally, brothers, whatever is true, whatever is noble, whatever is right, whatever is pure, whatever is lovely, whatever is admirable—if anything is excellent or praiseworthy—think about such things. Whatever you have learned or received or heard from me, or seen in me—put it into practice. And the God of peace will be with you." Philippians 4:8,9

BIBLICAL BASIS

Proverbs 3:5,6; Isaiah 55:9; John 8:32,44; 17:15,17; Romans 12:2; 2 Corinthians 10:3-5; Philippians 4:6-9; Colossians 3:15,16; James 1:8; 1 Peter 1:13

THE BIG IDEA

Strongholds are sinful patterns of thought and action that are deeply ingrained in our lives. Strongholds do not have to control us unless we let them. We have the power through Christ to discern Satan's lies, to confess and renounce our sins and to pull down strongholds with the truth of God's Word. We can win the battle for our minds in Jesus Christ.

AIMS OF THIS SESSION

During this session you will guide students to:
- Learn about and be able to identify some spiritual strongholds;
- Apply Scripture for pulling down strongholds;
- Discover how to take sinful thoughts captive while dwelling on pure thoughts.

KEY RESOURCES AND PREPARATION

- Read chapter 9 of *Stomping Out the Darkness*.
- Secure these supplies before the session: an interstate map of the U.S.A., newspapers, magazines, scissors, paste or glue, poster board (three to four pieces), felt pens, balloons (one for each person in the group), pencils, small pieces of paper (about 2x3 inches).

- Make copies of the worksheet "Pulling Down Strongholds" on page 55 for everyone in the group.
- Begin to identify your own strongholds and start pulling them down applying the teachings in this session to yourself. Pray for all of your students or group members.
- Have pencils and paper for everyone.

Getting Started (10 minutes)

Display an interstate map of the U.S.A. Tell each person they have two minutes to determine the best route from Chicago to San Francisco. After everyone has plotted a route, discuss:

How many different ways are there to get there?

Which way is the shortest and fastest?

How do the lower (southern) routes compare to the higher (northern) routes?

Explain: **On this map there is a high road along Interstate 80 and a low road along Interstate 40 to go to San Francisco. In the Christian life, there is also a "low road" and a "high road" for living—God's way versus man's way. Let's read Isaiah 55:9 and Proverbs 3:5,6. If we try to go back and forth between both ways, our spiritual growth will be blocked and we will be confused and unstable.** Read James 1:8. **The battle within us is between the low and high roads, God's way and man's. That battle is found in our minds. We are going to explore how to fight and win that battle.**

Getting Focused (10 minutes)

Give everyone in the group a pencil and paper. Ask them to write 2 Corinthians 10:3-5 on that piece of paper and to circle every word or phrase in the passage that refers to something that is part of war. For example, everyone will circle "weapons." Give everyone about three minutes to do this. Then ask the group to say the words that they have circled and list those words and phrases on a chalkboard or flip chart. That list should contain these words: world, wage war, weapons, fight, divine power, demolish, strongholds, knowledge of God, sets itself up against, take captive, make it obedient.

As a group, decide which words represent God's kingdom and the high road, and which words represent the low road, man's way and Satan's kingdom. Draw an arrow pointing up by each word that is God's way and an arrow pointing down by each word or phrase that is man's or Satan's way. Ask, **What is the prize of this battle for which we are fighting? What needs to be destroyed to capture this prize? What is a stronghold?**

Ask each person in the group to write 2 Corinthians 10:3 with the opposite hand they usually write with, i.e. right-handed people write with their left and vice versa. Then explain: **A stronghold is a bad pattern of thought burned into our minds either through repetition over time or through one-time, deeply shocking experiences. Just like we learned to write a certain way and now think that it's the correct way for us to write, so we learn certain thought habits that we do for so long that we think they are right, even when they are wrong. Let's explore how these strongholds develop in our minds.**

Getting into the Word (20 minutes)

Say: **Bad and destructive thoughts burned into our minds are strongholds. For example, hate and**

hostility are strongholds. What other strongholds can you think of? List suggestions from the group on the chalkboard. **Satan's lie about strongholds is that we have no control over them.** Read John 8:44. **In Scripture, God reveals the truth through Jesus Christ. In 2 Corinthians 10:3-5, we read that we can pull down strongholds. They do not have to control us. Satan's only power over us is what we give him. Our defense against Satan is God's Word, the truth.** Ask someone to read John 8:32 and John 17:15,17. **The Bible tells us how to pull down strongholds.** Distribute "Pulling Down Strongholds." **Everyone has five minutes to complete this study and then we will share as a whole group what we've discovered.**

After everyone has completed the worksheet, list these steps on the chalkboard:

Pulling Down Strongholds:

Step 1: Renew your mind

Step 2: Prepare your mind for action

Step 3: Take every thought captive

Step 4: Pray and turn to God (confess and renounce)

Have everyone check the order of steps on their worksheets with the order you gave them. Then ask:

How do we renew our minds? Look up Colossians 3:15,16.

What actions can we take to prepare our minds for attacks from Satan and the world?

What can we do when a thought pops into our minds that doesn't agree with the Word of God?

GETTING REAL (10 MINUTES)

Divide the students into three or four small groups. Give every group a poster board, glue or tape, magazines and newspapers to make a collage. Give these instructions: **Have someone in your group read aloud Philippians 4:8,9. On one side of your poster board have one person list the things our minds should dwell on as the Scripture is read. Have everyone in your group take a magazine or newspaper and look for pictures that would illustrate each thing on your list. Paste those picture on the same side of your poster board making a collage. Then have everyone find pictures that would illustrate what *not* to dwell upon with our minds. Make a collage of those pictures on the other side of your poster board.**

After the groups have made their collages, take a few minutes for each group to show both sides of their posters to the entire group and explain what they have chosen to paste on each side and why.

GETTING ARMED (5 MINUTES)

Have everyone take their worksheet and go to a quiet place in the room alone with the Lord. Have each person spend a few minutes in silent prayer seeking God's guidance and strength in praying about the steps they need to take in pulling down the strongholds they have circled.

Gather the whole group. Give everyone a balloon and small piece of paper. On that paper, ask everyone to write his or her name. Have everyone then take that piece of paper, put it inside the balloon and then blow up the balloon.

Have everyone stand in a circle and toss their balloons up in the air. See how long the group can keep all the balloons airborne. After a few moments of this, tell everyone to grab a balloon—not their own—and to pop it. They are to take the note inside and form a closing prayer circle praying silently for whomever's name they have. Now close the group with a group prayer that might be something like:

Heavenly Father, in the name of Jesus Christ we pull down these strongholds in our lives. Pause. **And agree with one another to take every thought captive for Jesus Christ. Amen.** Pause.

PULLING DOWN STRONGHOLDS

Look up each Scripture and then write next to it the specific action that that Scripture says to take to pull down a stronghold, sin-habit or destructive attitude or action in our lives.

Then, number the steps in order from the first step through the fourth step.

Order of Steps   Action to Take to Pull Down a Stronghold

_____ 1 Peter 1:13   ....

_____ Philippians 4:6,7   ....

_____ 2 Corinthians 10:5   ....

_____ Romans 12:2   ....

Here is a brief list of some strongholds:

Depression	Impure Thoughts	Lust
Inferiority	Gossip	Lying
Hypocrisy	Hatred	Dishonoring Parents
Idolatry	Jealousy	Immorality
Stealing	The Occult	Anger
Unforgiveness	Sexual Sin	Rebellion
Fear	Worry	

Circle a stronghold that you struggle to pull down.

Based on the steps for pulling down strongholds listed above, what specific steps do you need to take to pull this stronghold down?

1. ....

2. ....

3. ....

4. ....

HANDLING AND HEALING EMOTIONAL HURTS

KEY VERSES

"When I kept silent, my bones wasted away through my groaning all day long. Therefore let everyone who is godly pray to you while you may be found; surely when the mighty waters rise, they will not reach him." Psalm 32:3,6

"Search me, O God, and know my heart; test me and know my anxious thoughts. See if there be any offensive way in me, and lead me in the way everlasting." Psalm 139:23,24

"For if you forgive men when they sin against you, your heavenly Father will also forgive you. But if you do not forgive men their sins, your Father will not forgive your sins." Matthew 6:14,15

"Everyone should be quick to listen, slow to speak and slow to become angry, for man's anger does not bring about the righteous life that God desires." James 1:19,20

BIBLICAL BASIS

Genesis 50:15-21; Ruth 1:8-18; Psalm 32:3,6; 51:1-6; 109:8-13; 139:23,24; Isaiah 53:5,6; Lamentations 3:1-11,18-24; Matthew 6:14,15; John 12:42,43; Romans 12:15; 2 Corinthians 5:17; Ephesians 4:26; James 1:19,20

THE BIG IDEA

Instead of stuffing our feelings or letting our emotions all hang out, we can honestly acknowledge how we feel, confess our sin and forgive those who have hurt us emotionally in the past through the forgiving love of Jesus Christ.

AIMS OF THIS SESSION

During this session you will guide students to:
• Recognize that emotions are a warning system from God;
• Discover the importance of acknowledging emotions instead of "stuffing" them or "letting it all hang out";
• Take steps toward dealing with negative emotions and resolving hurts.

KEY RESOURCES AND PREPARATION

• Read chapters 10 and 11 in *Stomping Out the Darkness*.
• Make copies of the worksheets for everyone in the group: "Color Your Feelings" on page 61 and "Handling Our Emotions" on page 63.

- Before the session, make three sets of colored construction paper including these colors in each set: black, grey, brown, blue, green, red, yellow and white.
- Have a paper, pencils and wastepaper basket available for use in the session.
- Go through the 12 Steps to Forgiveness for yourself before the session.
- Pray for forgiveness for any hurt feelings you have been carrying from any persons in the group. Pray for God's Spirit to be at work during this session.

GETTING STARTED (10 MINUTES)

As people arrive, divide the students equally into three groups. Give each group a set of construction paper sheets.

Give everyone a copy of "Color Your Feelings." Instruct the groups: **Look at the colors your group has and match the colors with feelings. For example, yellow might represent feeling happy. List on your worksheets which colors match which feelings for your group. You have two minutes to do this.**

Sit in a circle. Starting with the tallest person in your group, share which colors you matched to which feelings. Go around the circle to the right so that each person can share his or her answers. Now as a group decide on a consensus of answers. Then go around the circle one more time sharing which weather forecast best fits you right now and why. You have five minutes to do this. GO!

As a whole group share how each small group matched their colors and feelings. Then on the chalkboard, write a matched list on which the whole group agrees.

GETTING FOCUSED (10 MINUTES)

Say to the group: **Feelings are neither good nor bad. They're just part of being human. Emotions are to our souls what physical feelings are to our bodies. They are God's emergency warning system to let us know what is going on inside. Emotions do not have to control us. Rather, beliefs based on God's truth which we obey can result in feelings that reflect God's view of our situations. Instead of letting our feelings dictate our beliefs and actions, they can be the result of obeying God's truth.**

At times, we might naturally feel one way about a circumstance when God's view might be very different. Let's see how that works. I will read you a situation. As a group, decide how most people would naturally feel about it. Have one person in your small group hold up the color of construction paper that reflects a natural feeling response to that situation. Then we'll see how God views it.

Situation One: The prophet Jeremiah was facing disease, the loss of his friends to death and exile, and terrible hardships. Read Lamentations 3:1-11,18. **Hold up the color representing how Jeremiah was naturally feeling.** Pause. **Now listen to what happened when God's perspective got hold of Jeremiah.** Read Lamentations 3:19-24. **What emotional response did God help Jeremiah to reach? Hold up the color you think it is?** Discuss as a group the colors (feelings) they held up.

Situation Two: Remember Joseph? His brothers plotted to kill him and then sold him into slavery in Egypt. Then Potiphar accused him of loving his wife and threw Joseph into jail. How do you think Joseph would have naturally felt about this? Pause for groups to hold up colors. Discuss why they chose those colors (feelings). **Now listen to what Joseph felt after he became a**

ruler in Egypt and asked his family to move to Egypt. Read Genesis 50:15-21. **Hold up the color you feel represents how God enabled Joseph to respond emotionally to his brothers.** Discuss the colors that are chosen and why.

Situation Three: Remember Ruth? Her father-in-law and husband died. Her mother-in-law, Naomi, wanted to leave Ruth behind and move to another country. How do you think Ruth might have naturally felt about this? Have groups hold up colors and then discuss why they chose those certain colors (feelings). **Here is how Ruth responded to Naomi.** Read Ruth 1:8-18. **Hold up the color (feeling) that God gave Ruth the strength to feel about her future with Naomi.** Discuss the colors chosen by the groups.

GETTING INTO THE WORD (15 MINUTES)

Give everyone in the group a copy of "Handling Our Emotions." Say to the whole group: **There are three ways to handle our emotions. These three options are listed on your worksheets. As a small group, have one person read the passage of Scripture and then choose which way you think the person having those feeling was handling their emotions. Take about seven minutes to complete your worksheets as small groups. Then we will discuss what you have discovered.**

After the groups have finished their worksheets, discuss which options the groups assigned to which Scriptures and why. Ask everyone to find a partner and to share:

Which option do you use the most? Why?

How many people do you have that you can honestly share your feelings with? Do you need more?

Pray for each other to be more open with self and God and a few other persons in acknowledging their true feelings.

Pray and ask God to reveal to your mind your true feelings.

GETTING REAL (10 MINUTES)

Say to the group: **Emotions that have been rooted in powerful, past memories are called** *primary emotions.* **Many of our primary emotions from the past lie hidden within us until something or someone triggers them. For example, the past memory of physical or verbal abuse may lay hidden within someone for years. But a present trauma might trigger the memory and primary emotion of hate, rage, fear or guilt from that past experience.**

A primary emotion from the past may be positive. If you had a loving father or mother, then positive feelings toward other authority or parental figures will be present. But if we have had negative primary emotions from the past, then we must learn how to resolve past problems or our hurt will keep building up within us.

Read Psalm 139:23,24. **Let's explore the positive ways we can handle hurtful memories and feelings from the past.** Write these statements on a chalkboard or flip chart or overhead projector. Ask someone to read the passage as you write the statement.

See Your Past in Light of Who You Are—2 Corinthians 5:17. Ask everyone in the group to say three times—louder each time—"I am a new creation in Christ."

Forgive Those Who Have Hurt You in the Past—Matthew 6:14,15. Pray and ask God to reveal to their minds those people they need to forgive. Give everyone a sheet of paper and ask them to make a list of people that God has revealed. They will not be sharing this list with anyone else but God.

Explain: **Forgiveness is not forgetting. Forgiveness is choosing not to bring up past sins and use them against others. Forgiveness does not tolerate another's sin. It's okay to forgive another's sin while at the same time confronting them with the truth about their sin in love. Forgiveness does not demand revenge or repayment for past hurts. You must choose whether to live in bitterness and resentment for another's sin against you or to obey God, forgive that person and live in peace with God, yourself and that person.**

With your list of people that you need to forgive, take these steps.

1. **Pray a prayer like this: "Dear heavenly father, I ask You now to bring to surface all the painful memories so that I can choose to forgive those people from my heart. I ask You, too, to bring to mind all the people I need to forgive. I pray this in the precious name of Jesus who has forgiven me and who will heal me from my hurts, amen." Then write their names or initials on your paper.**
2. **Next to their names write you feel about the people and their offenses.** Pause.
3. **Realize that the cross of Jesus makes forgiveness possible, right and fair. Read Isaiah 53:5,6.**
4. **Decide you will bear the burden of each person's sin deciding not to strike back or take revenge.**
5. **Decide to forgive.**
6. **Take your list to God and pray the following: I forgive** (name) **for** (list of offenses), **even though it made me feel** (express to God how it made you feel).
7. **Destroy the list.** Ask each person to fold up their list and then tear it up completely, throwing it away in the wastepaper basket in front of the group.
8. **Try to understand the people you have forgiven. They are victims also.**
9. **Do not expect that your decision to forgive will result in major changes in the other people. Instead, simply pray for God to work in their lives.**
10. **Expect positive results of forgiveness in you.**
11. **Thank God for the lessons you have learned and the maturity you have gained as a result of your decision to forgive.**
12. **Be sure to accept your part of the blame and confess any sin to God (if the Lord shows you that you were wrong, too).**

GETTING ARMED (5 MINUTES)

In your own words, retell the story of Corrie ten Boom on pp. 178-179 in chapter 11 of *Stomping Out the Darkness*. Then say: **Perhaps, you need to express the forgiveness you've extended to someone. Consider a way you might do that this week.**

COLOR YOUR FEELINGS

Match each feeling with the color you feel best represents that feeling. In the blank, write the feeling that best matches the color.

Colors	**Feelings**
.... Yellow	Depressed
.... Blue	Guilty
.... Green	Hopeful
.... Red	Sad
.... Black	Bored
.... White	Angry
.... Brown	Happy
.... Grey	Forgiven

If you were to choose a weather forecast to represent your feelings right now, what would it be?
Circle one.
Sunny
Partly cloudy
Scattered showers
Rain
Snow
Thunderstorms

HANDLING OUR EMOTIONS

Option 1: Stuffing Our Emotions
When we stuff our emotions, we attempt to bury our feelings. We cover up our true feelings and try to keep them from showing to others, ourselves or God.

Option 2: Letting It All Hang Out
When we let our emotions all hang out, we loose control and don't care what we say or do to others.

Option 3: Acknowledging Our Emotions
When we admit how we feel to ourselves and God, we get in touch with our emotions through being truthful with God and ourselves. We also find someone we trust with whom we can share and acknowledge our emotions openly and honestly without hurting them.

Read the following Scriptures. Then decide as a group which option best describes how that passage describes handling emotions.

Passage	Option
Psalm 32:3,6	
Psalm 51:1-6	
Psalm 109:8-13	
John 12:42,43	
Romans 12:15	
James 1:19,20; Ephesians 4:26	

Which option do you personally use the most?

Why?

DEALING WITH REJECTION AND BUILDING RELATIONSHIPS

KEY VERSES

"Blessed is the man who does not walk in the counsel of the wicked or stand in the way of sinners or sit in the seat of mockers. But his delight is in the law of the Lord, and on his law he meditates day and night. He is like a tree planted by streams of water, which yields its fruit in season and whose leaf does not wither. Whatever he does prospers." Psalm 1:1-3

"Who are you to judge someone else's servant? To his own master he stands or falls. And he will stand, for the Lord is able to make him stand." Romans 14:4

"So then, just as you received Christ Jesus as Lord, continue to live in him, rooted and built up in him, strengthened in the faith as you were taught, and overflowing with thankfulness." Colossians 2:6,7

BIBLICAL BASIS

Psalm 1:1-3; Romans 14:4; Colossians 2:6,7

THE BIG IDEA

We mature as disciples of Christ Jesus as the barren destructive roots are removed from our lives and as we walk according to the truth of who we are in Christ and grow in faith.

AIMS OF THIS SESSION

During this session you will guide students to:
- Avoid criticizing or judging others;
- Learn about God's plan for maturing as a disciple;
- Uncover barren roots in their lives and the lives of others;
- Commit to growing and maturing a fruitful life in Christ.

KEY RESOURCES AND PREPARATION

- Read and prepare to explain the contents of chapters 12 and 13 in *Stomping Out the Darkness*.
- Deal with the barren roots in your life, and do all the exercises in this session before you lead the group in doing them.
- Make copies of the worksheets for everyone: "How to Handle Being Critical" on page 69, "Discipling in Christ" on page 71, "Bearing Fruit for Christ" on page 73, "Who Am I?" on pages 23 and 25 and "Since I Am in Christ" on pages 27 and 29.
- Pray for each person in your group.
- Have a chalkboard or flip chart, chalk or felt pens, pencils and paper for group members.

Getting Started (10 minutes)

Once the group has arrived ask for three volunteers. Send those three volunteers out of the room telling them you will bring them back into the room in just a couple minutes. Once the three volunteers have left the room, instruct the rest of the group to get into groups of three or four people and begin sharing everything that happened to them last week. Tell them to share anything interesting and comfortable that happened to each of them last week starting with the tallest and going around the circle to the right.

Also say: **While you are sharing in your group about last week, do not let anyone else into your small group. As our three volunteers come back into the room, ignore them and do not talk to them. Start sharing.**

Now go and ask the volunteers to come back into the room. Tell them to join a small group and begin sharing and talking with the group. Let them try for about two minutes to break into a small group. Then discuss as a whole group:

How did those of you in the small groups feel about excluding and rejecting those who came back into the room?

What were those of you trying to break into small groups feeling?

What are some ways that we reject people or we get rejected every day? How do we handle rejection? If not suggested, then bring up defensiveness, rebellion, beating the system or giving into the system.

Getting Focused (10 minutes)

Ask the group to help you make a list on the chalkboard or flip chart of all the things they criticize in others. Make the list look like this:

Peers   Parents   Teachers   Authority Figures   Coaches

For example, peers may be criticized or judged for physical looks or athletic ability, clothes, hairstyle, others they associate with, the way they talk, morality, etc. Parents may be criticized for being too strict or lax, abusive, uninformed, old-fashioned, etc. Teachers may be criticized for being dumb, unorganized, too strict or lax, poor communicators, etc. Authority figures may be professionals, law enforcers, ministers, politicians, etc.

After making these lists, divide the room into four corners and label each corner with one of the above categories. Ask people to go and stand in the corner of the room of the group of people toward which they are most critical.

Give each person in each group a copy of "How to Handle Being Critical." Give these instructions: **Each person in the group is to complete the worksheet. Then discuss in pairs the questions at the bottom of the worksheet. You will have five minutes to do this. Go!**

Getting into the Word (20 minutes)

Say to the group: **Discipleship is a way to grow in our relationships with God and one another in the church. Caring and growing together as Christians is what being Christ's disciples is all about. Discipleship is the intensely personal activity of two or more persons helping each other experience a growing relationship with God. If being judgmental and critical allows darkness and division to come into the relationships of disciples, what will enable us to grow together as disciples?**

How does a person become a disciple and grow as one?

Give each person in the group a copy of "Discipling in Christ."

Explain Level I to the group using the background provided in chapter 13 of *Stomping Out the Darkness*. Have the group look up the Scripture references and different people read the reference aloud as you go through Level I. Divide the students into pairs. Ask them to share with their partner the completion to these sentences:

Fear of God means ....

Rebellion against God is ....

The greatest fear I have in trying to lead someone to Christ is ....

....

Explain Level II to the group and read Scripture passages as you did with Level I. Then have the pairs share:

The place in this level where I need to mature the most is ....

....

Then explain Level III to the group and have the Scriptures read. Again have the pairs share:

The place I need to grow the most in my walk with Christ is ....

....

GETTING REAL (10 MINUTES)

Now give all the pairs copies of "Bearing Fruit for Christ." Read Psalm 1:1-3 for the group. Read the following statements to the pairs and ask them to identify the root in a barren life that is reflected by the statement. After group members seek to guess the root, tell them the correct answer and go on to the next.

Statement	Barren Root
"I can't do anything right."	False Belief System
"I feel out of place. Nobody loves me."	Rejection
"I know what I should do. I just don't want to do it."	Rebellion
"I'm afraid to try anything. I might fail."	Fear
"I can't get over how I've been hurt."	Unforgiveness

Discuss:

What other statements might someone make that would reflect a barren root system in their spiritual lives?

What are some of the questions you might ask a person, to expose what kind of root structure that person has? Share some of the questions suggested in chapter 13 of *Stomping Out the Darkness*, pp. 206-208.

Say to the group and write on a chalkboard or flip chart: **After a root issue is uncovered, 1. Encourage emotional honesty; 2. Share the truth; 3. Call for a response; 4. Help them plan for the future.** Briefly explain what each action involves.

GETTING ARMED (5 MINUTES)

Give everyone a copy of "Who Am I?" and "Since I Am in Christ." Ask each person to choose five statements that reflect where they are right now in their spiritual maturity and circle them. Ask them to choose five statements that reflect what they need to grow and write an exclamation mark (!) beside them. Then they should share what they have marked with their partners.

Instruct them to look at the barren tree and identify one root that needs to be removed from his or her life, then to look at the fruitful tree and identify one root that needs to grow in his or her life. Then each individual should pray for themselves with their partners agreeing with them.

Pray this way: **Father, thank You for Your work in my life. May the root of**...................................

...................**be removed from my life and the root of**...

grow to meet my needs. In Jesus' name, amen.

How to Handle Being Critical

When you are critical of someone else, how are you thinking and feeling? Put an X on the line where it would best describe you.

When I am critical or judgmental of others, I:

1. ....
   Want to win at all costs   Try to control others

2. ....
   Feel like something is wrong with me   Feel rejected

3. ....
   Feel inferior   Feel superior

4. ....
   Am being defensive   Feel my rights have been violated

Positive ways to react to others instead of being critical are:

Rate yourself for each statement. 4 = "I do this often," 3 = "I do this sometimes," 2 = "I do this rarely," 1 = "I never do this."

_____ 1. Treating others like family instead of enemies.

_____ 2. Focusing on my character development instead of their character weaknesses.

_____ 3. Trying to meet the needs of others instead of just getting my needs met.

_____ 4. Looking at my responsibilities in a relationship instead of my rights.

_____ 5. Allowing the Holy Spirit to convict others instead of trying to do that myself.

_____ 6. Speaking the truth in love to others instead of attacking them and judging them.

_____ Total

Scores: 20-24 = You are doing super. Guard against pride.

15-19 = You are growing in your relationships.

10-14 = You are doing okay but need some real work in not being too critical of others.

9 or under = Others may be distancing themselves from you because you are too critical.

What do you need to work on the most in the way you criticize others? ....

....

What positive way to react to others do you do best? What do you need to work on the most?

....

....

DISCIPLING IN CHRIST

LEVELS OF CONFLICT AND GROWTH

	LEVEL I:	LEVEL II:	LEVEL III:
	Identity: Complete in Christ (Colossians 2:10)	**Maturity:** Built up in Christ (Colossians 2:7)	**Walk:** Walk in Christ (Colossians 2:6)
SPIRITUAL LIFE	**Conflict:** Lack of salvation or assurance (Ephesians 2:1-3)	**Conflict:** Walking according to the flesh (Galatians 5:19-21)	**Conflict:** Insensitive to the Spirit's leading (Hebrews 5:11-14)
	Growth: Child of God (1 John 3:1-3; 5:11-13)	**Growth:** Walking according to the Spirit (Galatians 5:22,23)	**Growth:** Led by the Spirit (Romans 8:14)
MIND	**Conflict:** Darkened understanding (Ephesians 4:18)	**Conflict:** Wrong beliefs of philosophy of life (Colossians 2:8)	**Conflict:** Pride (1 Corinthians 8:1)
	Growth: Renewed mind (Romans 12:2; Ephesians 4:23)	**Growth:** Handling accurately the Word of truth (2 Timothy 2:15)	**Growth:** Adequate, equipped for every good work (2 Timothy 3:16,17)
EMOTIONS	**Conflict:** Fear (Matthew 10:26-33)	**Conflict:** Anger (Ephesians 4:31), anxiety (1 Peter 5:7), depression (2 Corinthians 4:1-18)	**Conflict:** Discouragement and sorrow (Galatians 6:9)
	Growth: Freedom (Galatians 5:1)	**Growth:** Joy, peace, patience (Galatians 5:22)	**Growth:** Contentment (Philippians 4:11)
WILL	**Conflict:** Rebellion (1 Timothy 1:9)	**Conflict:** Lack of self-control, compulsive (1 Corinthians 3:1-3)	**Conflict:** Undisciplined (2 Thessalonians 3:7,11)
	Growth: Submissive (Romans 13:1,2)	**Growth:** Self-control (Galatians 5:23)	**Growth:** Disciplined (1 Timothy 4:7,8)
RELATION-SHIPS	**Conflict:** Rejection (Ephesians 2:1-3)	**Conflict:** Unforgiveness (Colossians 3:1-3)	**Conflict:** Selfishness (Philippians 2:1-5; 1 Corinthians 10:24)
	Growth: Acceptance (Romans 5:8; 15:7)	**Growth:** Forgiveness (Ephesians 4:32)	**Growth:** Brotherly love (Romans 12:10; Philippians 2:1-5)

Dealing with Rejection and Building Relationships

BEARING FRUIT FOR CHRIST

BARREN LIFE

REJECTION
REBELLION
FEAR UNFORGIVENESS FALSE BELIEF SYSTEM

FRUITFUL LIFE

PRUNING
PRUNING
CHALLENGING ENCOURAGING
FEEDING INSTRUCTING
FREEDOM SUBMISSION
ACCEPTANCE TRUE BELIEF SYSTEM
FORGIVENESS

COLOSSIANS 2:6,7
Figure 13-B

FREE AT LAST!

KEY VERSES

"It is for freedom that Christ has set us free. Stand firm, then, and do not let yourselves be burdened again by a yoke of slavery." Galatians 5:1
"We will in all things grow up into him who is the Head, that is, Christ." Ephesians 4:15
Read Romans 7,8.

BIBLICAL BASIS

Isaiah 14:12; Matthew 5:21-30,43-48; 6:9,25-34; 8:16,17,28,29; 9:28-34; 10:1; 16:16,24-27; Mark 3:11-12; 9:17-27; Luke 2:13; 5:18-25; 10:18,38-42; John 1:1; 2:14-16; 4:6-26; 5:2-9; 8:34-38,42-47; 11:43,44; 12:31,42; Acts 2:4; Romans 7,8; 2 Corinthians 11:14; Galatians 2:20; 5:1; Ephesians 2:2; 4:15,16; 6:11,12; 1 Timothy 4:8; 2 Timothy 1:7; Hebrews 11:24-26; 1 Peter 5:8; Revelation 5:5; 20:10

THE BIG IDEA

As a young person, Christ can set you free from bondages so that you can walk with God and your unique identity can be established in Him.

AIMS OF THIS SESSION

During this session you will guide students to:
- Explore key biblical passages;
- Uncover some bondages that many young people face;
- Distinguish between the natural and supernatural, the religious and worldly realms.

KEY RESOURCES AND PREPARATION

- The introduction and chapters 1-3 of *The Bondage Breaker Youth Edition*.
- You will need these supplies: masking tape, felt pens, chalkboard or flip chart, pencils and paper, self-adhesive name tags, newsprint, adding machine tape, trash sack.
- Read all of the Scripture passages in this session.
- Using 3x5-inch cards, write the following Scripture references on cards (one reference on each card): John 5:2-9; John 12:42; 2 Timothy 1:7; Matthew 9:28-34; Luke 5:18-25; John 2:14-16; John 4:6-26; Mark 9:17-27; Mark 3:11-12; Matthew 5:21-26; Matthew 5:27-30; Matthew 5:43-48; Matthew 8:16,17; John 8:42-47; John 8:34-38; Matthew 6:25-34.
- Tape up three sheets of newsprint, with each labeled with one of the following titles: Physical Bondages, Emotional and Intellectual Bondages, Spiritual Bondages.
- Make copies of the worksheet "The Truth About Bondages and Freedom" on page 81 for everyone.

• Pray by name for each person that will be involved in this session. Pray for yourself. Find a prayer partner to pray with and agree with you each week as you prepare to lead the upcoming session. You might prepare in prayer for each session by reading Ephesians 6:10-18 and then praying through that passage arming yourself with God's armor.

GETTING STARTED (10 MINUTES)

As youth enter, put a name tag on the back of each person. Before the session you will have written the following on different name tags.

Name	**Scripture Reference**
Satan	Luke 10:18
Lucifer	Isaiah 14:12
Devil	Revelation 20:10
Beelzebub	Matthew 12:24
Demons	Matthew 8:28,29
Evil Spirits	Matthew 10:1
Angel of Light	2 Corinthians 11:14
Angels	Luke 2:13
Holy Spirit	Acts 2:4
Son of God	Matthew 16:16
Word of God	John 1:1
Prince of This World	John 12:31
Prince of the Air	Ephesians 2:2
Rulers of Darkness	Ephesians 6:12
Roaring Lion	1 Peter 5:8
Lion of Judah	Revelation 5:5
Heavenly Father	Matthew 6:9
Armor of God	Ephesians 6:11

Each young person is told: **You may ask anyone in the room a question about who you are. You may not ask, "Who am I?" Rather, ask about the name tag on your back with such questions as, "Am I good?" "Do I help?" "Do I attack?" You may only ask questions that can be answered with yes or no.**

Take three to five minutes for this to happen and then stop the exercise. Those who have not guessed who they are may be told. Have everyone take the name tag off of their backs and put it on the piece of newsprint that best fits its category. The two pieces of newsprint are labeled:

The Kingdom of God   The Kingdom of Satan

If any of the name tags are put under the wrong category, have young person read the Scripture for that name and have them move the name tag.

As a group, ask: **Which ones are unfamiliar or have you never heard of before?** Have youth say any names on the list that they do not know. Then go back through the list having youth in the group read the Scripture passages that correspond to any of the names that have one or more votes next to them.

Getting Focused (10 Minutes)

Ask for six volunteers from the group. Divide the volunteers into pairs. Ask one person from each pair to be the "disabled" volunteer. Number the pairs from one to three. Handicap each pair as follows:

Pair 1—Tie one person's hands behind him or her.
Pair 2—Blindfold one person.
Pair 3—Bind one person's foot to his or her hand.

The person who is "disabled" or "bound up" is then instructed to feed the other person a donut or give that person a drink of water. No verbal communication is allowed between the pair. Have the pairs attempt this one pair at a time. After all have tried, discuss:

How did the handicapped or bound people feel?

How did those being fed the donut or being given a drink of water feel?

The group leader now explains: **There are many kinds of bondages in life. One kind is physical. Another is emotional—like fear. Another might be mental—like low self-image. Another might be spiritual—like idolatry. Find two or three other people and form a circle.**

Getting Into the Word (20 Minutes)

Divide the students into trios. Give each trio two or three of the 3x5-inch cards that were prepared before the session. Ask them to look up the passages on the cards and then to decide the kind of bondage each passage describes. Give these instructions: **Look up each passage. Use a felt pen to write a word or short phrase on the back of the card that describes the bondage like fear, demonization, disease, etc. Then write, "Jesus sets us free by ...." and fill in how Jesus set the person or people free in the passage. For example, if the bondage is disease, "Jesus sets us free by healing us."**

Give all the trios five minutes to do this. Then have each trio have the person whose birthday is most recent report back to the whole group what they found. On a chalkboard or flip chart, write the passage reference, the kind of bondage and the way Jesus sets us free.

Your listing may look something like this:

Reference	Bondage	Jesus' Freedom
John 5:2-9	Physical handicap	Healed
John 12:42; 2 Timothy 1:7	Fear	Power, love and a sound mind
Matthew 9:28-34	Demonized	Tells them to go
Luke 5:18-25	Paralysis	Forgiven and healed
John 2:14-16	Religious bondage	Cleanses
John 4:6-26	Immoral living	Reveals to her the truth
Mark 9:17-27	Demonized by a deaf and dumb spirit	Commands it to leave
Mark 3:11,12	Evil spirits attack	Silences them
Matthew 5:21-26	Hatred	Forgiveness
Matthew 5:27-30	Lust	Avoid it
Matthew 5:43-48	Hatred for enemies	Love for others
Matthew 8:16,17	Demonization	Drives evil spirits out with His Word

John 8:42-47	Lies	Truth
John 8:34-38	Slavery to Sin	Freedom
Matthew 6:25-34	Worry	Provides for us

Now distribute copies of "The Truth About Bondages and Freedom" to each trio. Tell the group: **As a trio, help one another complete just the True/False sections of your worksheets. You have two minutes and then I will give you the correct answers.** After two minutes, discuss the answers and explain any questions the group has about the statements. (Answers: 1. True; 2. False; 3. False; 4. False; 5. False; 6. False.)

Call the group's attention to the figure in the middle of their worksheets. Explain to them what it means to live in the "excluded middle" from *The Bondage Breaker Youth Edition*, pp. 37-38. Then have them do the matching exercise at the bottoms of their worksheets. (Answers: F, D, A, E, B, C.)

After sharing as a group the correct answers, read Romans 7:15-25 and Romans 8:1,2 to the group. Write these statements on the chalkboard or flip chart.

1. I can be free from the power of sin.
2. I can win the battle for my mind.

Have a group discussion on these questions:

How do these Scriptures say I can be free from sin? Win the battle for my mind?

What does the world or my flesh do to try to stop me from having victory over temptation and sin?

GETTING REAL (5 MINUTES)

Give each trio a roll of adding machine tape, a few pieces of masking tape and some felt pens, pens or pencils. Instruct them: **Unwind seven or eight feet of tape so that everyone in your small group can write on a section of tape without looking at what others are writing at the same time. You will not be sharing what you are writing with anyone else. First, write on your section of the adding machine tape the five things from which Christ has set you free from in the world of religion or the senses.** Pause. **Now, write one thing that really has you bound up today from which you need Jesus to set you free.** Pause. **Finally, write one bondage in someone else's life—a family member, friend, teacher, church member—from which that person needs to be set free.** Pause.

Have the shortest person stand in the middle of your group. One of you turn the written side of the tape toward that person and begin wrapping that person in the tape like they're a dead mummy. The other person helps wrap that person up in the tape of bondages. Use your masking tape to help keep the adding machine tape in place. Wait until everyone is finished.

Jesus sets us free from the deadly bondages that wrap us and bind up our lives. Everyone join me in declaring, "Jesus sets us free!" and rip off the bondages on your mummy.

When everyone has set their people free from the adding machine tape, pick up the entire mess of torn tape and place it in a trash sack in the center of your room. Gather the entire group in a circle around the trash sack.

GETTING ARMED (5 MINUTES)

Join hands in your circle. Invite everyone, beginning with yourself and going around to the right, to complete this simple prayer: **I thank You, Jesus, for setting me free from** ....

After everyone has prayed, you close the prayer time by praying a simple prayer that may be like this, having the entire group repeat each phrase after you: **Lord Jesus.** Pause. **You are my freedom.** Pause. **You can set me free from every bondage.** Pause. **You free me from fear.** Pause. **And give me a spirit of power.** Pause. **Love and a sound mind.** Pause. **Thank you, Lord. Amen.** Pause.

Before leaving, share with the group: **Next time, you will discover the courage you need to overcome bondages and problems in your life. I will be praying for you.**

Let youth know that if they would like to go through the Steps to Freedom privately, someone is available.

The Truth About Bondages and Freedom

Write *T* for true or *F* for false before each statement according to how you believe.

_____ 1. Demons were active when Christ was on earth and are still present and active today.

_____ 2. What early Christians called demonic activity is only mental illness.

_____ 3. Some problems are psychological and some are spiritual.

_____ 4. Christians can't be attacked by demonic forces.

_____ 5. The activity of demons is only seen in weird behavior or gross sin.

_____ 6. Freedom from spiritual bondage is the result of a power encounter with demonic forces.

The Excluded Middle

Unseen World Forces of God and Spiritual Forces	Religion
Excluded Middle	
Seen World of the Senses	Science

The View from the Cross

Match the text with the statement that most fits it. These are Jesus' guidelines for viewing life from the cross, from His perspective, instead of from the world's or a religious perspective.

_____ Matthew 16:24-27   A. Sacrifice the lower life to gain the higher life.

_____ Galatians 2:20   B. By the Spirit, die to your sinful desires.

_____ 1 Timothy 4:8   C. Sacrifice today's pleasures to gain God's reward.

_____ Luke 10:38-42   D. Be crucified with Christ.

_____ Romans 8:13,14   E. Choose the most important and meaningful.

_____ Hebrews 11:24-26   F. Deny yourself and pick up your cross.

YOUR AUTHORITY IN CHRIST

KEY VERSES

"When Jesus had called the Twelve together, he gave them power and authority to drive out all demons and to cure diseases, and he sent them out to preach the kingdom of God and to heal the sick." Luke 9:1,2

"And I have given you authority over all the power of the Enemy....However, the important thing is not that demons obey you, but that your names are registered as citizens of heaven." Luke 10:19,20 (*TLB*)

Read Ephesians 6:10-18.

BIBLICAL BASIS

Joshua 1:6,7; Matthew 12:29; 28:18; Mark 9:23; Luke 9:1,2; 10:19,20; Ephesians 1:18-20; 2:6; 5:21; 6:10-18; James 4:7; 1 John 5:14,15

THE BIG IDEA

As disciples of Jesus Christ, we have in Christ the authority and power to defeat Satan and his demons. Through prayer, we can claim Christ's authority to bind the strong man and see others and ourselves set free from bondages through Jesus Christ.

AIMS OF THIS SESSION

During this session you will guide students to:
- Learn that they have Christ's authority and power over Satan;
- Become familiar with the armor of God;
- Pray for binding the strong man and for Christ freeing others from bondages.

KEY RESOURCES AND PREPARATION

- Read chapters 4 and 5 of *The Bondage Breaker Youth Edition.*
- Prepare 3x5-inch cards for everyone in the group. Vary the assortment so that there are an equal number of cards with each of the following military ranks written on them. Thus with four different ranks and twenty in your group, then five would be generals, five would be captains and so forth: General, Captain, Sergeant, Private. Also have a chalkboard or flip chart, chalk or felt pens, pencils, rope and some small cups for water.
- Make copies of the worksheets for everyone: "God's Armor" on page 87 and "Binding the Strong Man" on page 89.
- Pray for each group member particularly focusing on any bondages that you see in their lives. Arm yourself daily with God's armor.

Getting Started (10 minutes)

As each person enters the room give them a 3x5-inch card with his or her rank written on it.

They are listed in the order of their authority from top to bottom. Write this list on the chalkboard and give these instructions: **Each of the military ranks listed on the board carry with it a certain amount of authority. On your cards is the rank that you are right now. You may go up to anyone in the room and give them a command if you are in rank above them in authority. You are in authority over everyone below you on the list. Here are the commands you are allowed to give: "Sit down." "Do not speak for one minute." "Stand up." "Go get me a cup of water."**

If you try to give a command to someone above you in rank, you must stop and take a command from them. We will do this for three minutes. Go!

Now discuss the following with the whole group:

How did you feel having to take orders from others? How did the generals feel not having to take orders from anyone?

What attitudes have to be in place for authority to work? When does authority break down? What is the difference between power and authority?

Getting Focused (10 minutes)

Say to the group: **As disciples of Jesus Christ, we have both the power and the authority over Satan and his demons.** Read Luke 9:1,2; 10:19,20. **Authority is the right to rule, while power is the ability to rule. We do not have in ourselves the spiritual power and authority over darkness but in Christ we do.**

Choose four people of about equal size and strength. Give them a rope and invite them to have a tug-of-war seeing which is the strongest. Now ask the group to arrange the teams on the tug-of-war that would most closely resemble the Christian's conflict against Satan. The group might put three people on one side and only one on the other. Or, they might put everyone on one side with nothing on the Enemy's side. Then discuss with the group:

Is spiritual conflict more like a tug-of-war or commanding with the authority of rank like we did in the first exercise?

After a discussion, explain to the group: **Spiritual authority is not a tug-of-war but rather it's a chain of command. Jesus has all power and authority according to Matthew 28:18. So with His name, authority and power, Satan and his demons are subject to the authority Christ has given us. Since we are in Christ as the Bible teaches, then His authority is in us.** Read Ephesians 1:18-20; 2:6. **How then do we exercise our power and authority in Christ? Let's look up four Scriptures and see what they tell us.** List these references on the board: Mark 9:23; James 4:7; Joshua 1:6,7; Ephesians 5:21. **Let's look each of these up and then see what it tells us about exercising spiritual authority.**

After having someone read each verse, discuss what the group sees in the text as instructions or commands to us. After each discussion, list these points by the texts.

Mark 9:23	1. Believe what God says.
James 4:7	2. Submit to God. Resist the devil and he will flee.
Joshua 1:6,7	3. Be strong, courageous and bold.
Ephesians 5:21	4. Depend on Christ and other Christians to help you.

GETTING INTO THE WORD (20 MINUTES)

Say to the group: **Things don't always go easy for Christians. Sometimes we are involved in spiritual conflict and are attacked by the Enemy. Remember, the only power Satan has is deception. Deception is not just a lie. It's a lie that's so close to the truth that you want to believe it. For example, if I tell you that I'm 12 feet tall you know that's a lie. You can see that I'm not. But if I tell you that I'm 5 feet 10 inches, you would probably believe me. That's a lie or deception because I'm really only 5 feet 9 1/2 inches. See the difference? He and his demons are deceivers. But Jesus Christ is Truth and His truth sets us free.** Distribute copies of "God's Armor" to everyone.

Ask everyone to complete the worksheets giving about three minutes for this. After everyone has completed their worksheet, discuss each piece of the armor:

What is the purpose of this part of the armor?

Which part of the armor do you feel the most need for right now? Why?

GETTING REAL (10 MINUTES)

Say to the group: **One of Satan's main weapons is to deceive and blind us. The primary weapon in combating this is prayer.** Read 1 John 5:14,15 to the group. **One way we can pray is to bind the strong man.** Have a group member read Matthew 12:29. **We can pray to bind Satan and be freed from the bondages he puts on our lives.**

Give everyone in the group a copy of "Binding the Strong Man." Say: **On this worksheet, list areas of your life that may be under attack. Pray that God binds the strong man and frees you from the bondages he may have on you. You have the authority and power in Christ to do that. Take the next five minutes in prayer for yourself, and bind Satan.**

Tell everyone to tear up their list and throw it away to symbolize the liberating power of Jesus Christ to set us free from the strong man and his bondages.

GETTING ARMED (5 MINUTES)

As a closing, have everyone stand up facing you. Say: **We are going to put on our armor symbolically right now. You might do this every morning for the next week to remind you to put on the covering of Jesus Christ each day before you do anything else.** Make motions like you are putting on each piece of armor. Have the group follow your motions and fill in the blanks.

Put on the belt of .... **by choosing to believe what God says in His Word.**

The breastplate of .... **by accepting that in Christ I'm righteous and by choosing today to walk righteously in the power of the Holy Spirit.**

The shoes of .... **by believing I'm at peace with God in Christ and by choosing to be a peacemaker today.**

The shield of .... **by trusting God no matter what happens to me today.**

The helmet of .... by thanking God for the gift of
eternal life that will never be taken from me.

The sword of the .... which is the Word of

.... by committing myself to answer every lie of the

devil today with the spoken Word of God.

Don't leave home without it!

GOD'S ARMOR

In the following Scripture from Ephesians 6:10-13, circle or highlight every *verb* in the text.

Finally, (be) strong in the Lord and in his mighty power. (Put) on the full armor of God so that you can take your stand against the devil's schemes. For our struggle is not against flesh and blood, but against the rulers, against the authorities, against the powers of this dark world and against the spiritual forces of evil in the heavenly realms. Therefore put on the full armor of God, so that when the day of evil comes, you may be able to stand your ground, and after you have done everything, to stand.

Below is pictured a soldier ready for battle. Read Ephesians 6:14-18 and label from the text each piece of the armor.

BINDING THE STRONG MAN

Read Matthew 12:29. List the persons you know that may be bound or under attack by Satan and the bondage they need freedom from. Make sure you pray about what you know to be *true*, not just a rumor you may have heard about them. A list of bondages is provided just to remind you of some.

Satan's bondages: Deceit, Disease, Fear, Anger, Addiction, Death, Pride, the Occult, Sexual Immorality

Name	Bondage	Prayer

RESISTING DEMONS AND THE OCCULT

KEY VERSES

"You must be very careful lest you be corrupted by the horrible customs of the nations now living there. For example, any Israeli who presents his child to be burned to death as a sacrifice to heathen gods, must be killed. No Israeli may practice black magic, or call on the evil spirits for aid, or be a fortune teller, or be a serpent charmer, medium, or wizard, or call forth the spirits of the dead. Anyone doing these things is an object of horror and disgust to the Lord, and it is because the nations do these things that the Lord your God will displace them. You must walk blamelessly before the Lord your God." Deuteronomy 18:9-13 (*TLB*)
"When an evil spirit comes out of a man, it goes through arid places seeking rest and does not find it. Then it says, 'I will return to the house I left.' When it arrives, it finds the house swept clean and put in order. Then it goes and takes seven other spirits more wicked than itself, and they go in and live there. And the final condition of that man is worse than the first." Luke 11:24-26
Read Mark 5:1-20.

BIBLICAL BASIS

Deuteronomy 18:9-13; 1 Samuel 15:12-26; 16:14,23; 1 Chronicles 9:33; 21:1; 23:5; Matthew 16:21-23; Mark 5:1-20; Luke 11:24-26; Acts 5:3; 2 Timothy 2:25,26

THE BIG IDEA

Demons are active in accusing, tempting and lying to Christians. Christians have the power to resist demonic activity and must resist the occult by using God's Word, the power of prayer and the encouraging strength of singing hymns and spiritual songs.

AIMS OF THIS SESSION

During this session you will guide students to:
- Recognize demonic activity, attacks, accusations and lies;
- Understand what demons do and how to resist temptation;
- Avoid the occult and seek freedom from it for themselves and their friends.

KEY RESOURCES AND PREPARATION

- Read chapters 7 and 8 in *The Bondage Breaker Youth Edition*.
- Make copies of the worksheet "The Personality of Demons" on page 95 for everyone in the group.
- Before the youth arrive, put up four large pieces of newsprint or poster board around the room and have

felt pens for four groups to write on the newsprint or poster board. At the top of each, write the word "Demons."

- Write the prayers from "Getting Real" on the chalkboard or flip cart before the session.
- Have pencils and papers for group members.
- Pray for each group member binding any occult power they may have opened themselves up to in the present or past. Purify your own life of these bondages as well.

GETTING STARTED (5 MINUTES)

As young people arrive, divide them into four groups assigned to the four pieces of newsprint you have put around the room. Each group needs a felt pen for writing on the newsprint.

When most everyone has arrived, give this assignment: **You have two minutes to list everything about demons that you know or have experienced—every action they take, personality characteristic, appearance, anything you know about demons. Go!**

After two minutes, stop the groups and say: **Now you have one minute to list words or phrases that explain why some people get involved with demons or satanic practices. For example, they may want spiritual power or knowledge. Go!**

After you stop the groups, ask each group to share what they have written on their newsprint about demons and why people get involved with evil spirits.

GETTING FOCUSED (10 MINUTES)

Keep the groups together. Give everyone a copy of "The Personality of Demons." Give these instructions: **Pull around into a circle in your groups. Have everyone read Luke 11:24-26; Mark 5:1-20. As a group, answer the True/False test. In a few minutes, I will give you the answers and then you can evaluate what you have written on your newsprint or poster.** (Answers: 1. True; 2. True; 3. False; 4. True; 5. False; 6. True; 7. True; 8. True.)

Discuss as a whole group what has been crossed off of the newsprint lists. Explain: **Demons lie and deceive. They want us to think they have more power or abilities than they do. But greater is He who is in us than he who is the world.**

GETTING INTO THE WORD (20 MINUTES)

Explain to the group: **The main activity of demons in our lives is to tempt and lie to us and try to plant thoughts in our minds to slow down or stop our maturing as disciples of Jesus Christ** (see 1 Chronicles 21:1; Matthew 16:21-23; Acts 5:3; 2 Timothy 2:25,26). **When we start to listen to their temptations, we move into increasing levels of bondage. At first, a Christian may live a fairly normal Christian life on the outside, but be wrestling with sinful thoughts on the inside. Without repentance, some Christians hear "evil" voices that seem to overpower their own thoughts. They think they may be going crazy and do not tell others of their struggles. Most of these Christians are depressed, anxious, paranoid, fearful, bitter or angry and may fall into addictive, destructive habits. The last level is when a Christian loses all control and lets these voices tell him or her what to do and think. These people stay at home, wander the streets and may end up in a mental institution. When temptation comes from demons, what should the Christian do? In your groups,** come up with what you believe are the best ways to respond to demonic temptations, accusations and deceptions.

Give the groups about three minutes to discuss this. Then as a whole group discuss:

Would you ever argue or discuss something with a demon? Why not?

Could a demon ever be right? You may discuss that a demon could be correct in telling someone the details of a past sin but is always wrong when telling us anything about our relationship with God or ourselves.

How did Jesus respond to demons? Can we respond simply by saying NO! and refusing to listen? Do we have the power to say no? Can we tell them to leave?

Have someone in the group read Deuteronomy 18:9-13, preferably from *The Living Bible*.

In your groups, make a list of all the things you know about today in our culture or world that are from the occult and evil spirits like satanism and seances. You have two minutes to do this.

When the groups have finished, make a master list on the chalkboard of all the things happening in our culture and world that are from the occult. Discuss:

How widespread are some of these things in our town? Our schools?

Do you know people who are involved in these practices? How are we to treat them? How should we respond to what they are doing in the occult? Are some Christians partaking in these practices? For example, how many know their zodiac sign and what it means?

Why do people get involved in the occult? (Suggest hidden knowledge and power.)

What is the problem with experimenting with the occult? Playing with tarot cards, Ouija boards or occult games?

You might share the some results from the survey taken at the start of the study.

Getting Real (10 minutes)

Have everyone read 1 Samuel 15:12-26; 16:14,23; 1 Chronicles 9:33; 23:5. Explain the evil spirit that Saul had and how God sent it upon Saul. Read *The Bondage Breaker Youth Edition*, pp. 118-121.

Discuss:

How did David use music? How was it used in the house of God?

Does Satan use music today to try to attack and deceive people? What are some of the music groups that are controlled by Satan?

Do you have any music or anything of the occult in your possession at home? What do you need to do about it?

At this point, invite everyone to get with a partner and to confess any time that they may have played with or seriously used something from the occult. Write these prayers on the chalkboard. Have the pairs pray this way: **Almighty God, I confess my use of**..
....**I renounce the power of Satan in my life. I ask for forgiveness in the blood of Jesus Christ. In Jesus' name, amen.**

If neither person has used anything from the occult in the present or past, then they may pray this prayer for someone they know who has: **Almighty God, we pray for**...........................**and his/her use of**..**. Convict them by the power of the Holy Spirit to stop using**..**. We bind you, Satan. We stand in our authority in Christ over all the powers of darkness and ask You, Lord, to protect and rescue**..**. In Jesus' name, amen.**

GETTING ARMED (5 MINUTES)

Close this session with singing songs like David had the Israelites do in the house of God. Some of the choruses you may wish to sing are: "Holy Ground," "Spirit of the Living God," "All Hail the Power of Jesus' Name," "Amazing Grace," "O Come All Ye Faithful," "Purify My Heart," "Majesty," "Mighty Warrior," "Holy, Holy, Holy," "Lord, You're Beautiful," "I Bow My Knee."

THE PERSONALITY OF DEMONS

Read Luke 11:24-26 and Mark 5:1-20. As a group decide if each statement is true or false. Write *T* for true or *F* for false before each statement.

_____ 1. Demons can exist outside or inside humans or animals.

_____ 2. Demons are able to travel at will.

_____ 3. Demons can communicate with each other but not with humans.

_____ 4. Each demon has a separate identity.

_____ 5. Demons have no memory or planning ability.

_____ 6. Demons are able to evaluate and make decisions.

_____ 7. Demons are able to combine forces.

_____ 8. Demons vary in degrees of wickedness.

After the leader gives you the answers, evaluate what your group has written on the newsprint. Cross through anything about demons that isn't verified by what you have discovered in the Bible.

ACCEPT CONVICTION; REFUSE ACCUSATION

KEY VERSES

"No temptation has seized you except what is common to man. And God is faithful; he will not let you be tempted beyond what you can bear. But when you are tempted, he will also provide a way out so that you can stand up under it." 1 Corinthians 10:13

"Yet now I am happy, not because you were made sorry, but because your sorrow led you to repentance. For you became sorrowful as God intended and so were not harmed in any way by us. Godly sorrow brings repentance that leads to salvation and leaves no regret, but worldly sorrow brings death." 2 Corinthians 7:9,10

"Do not love the world, nor the things in the world. If anyone loves the world, the love of the Father is not in him. For all that is in the world, the lust of the flesh and the lust of the eyes and the boastful pride of life, is not from the Father, but is from the world. And the world is passing away, and also its lusts; but the one who does the will of God abides forever." 1 John 2:15-17 (*NASB*)

Read Zechariah 3:1-10.

BIBLICAL BASIS

Zechariah 3:1-10; Matthew 4:3,6,8,9; 27:1-9; Luke 22:1-6,33,34; John 21:15-17; 1 Corinthians 10:13; 2 Corinthians 7:9,10; Philippians 4:8; 1 John 2:15-17

THE BIG IDEA

In Christ, we have the power to resist temptation, to receive conviction for our sin from the Holy Spirit, to resist Satan's accusations and to experience the forgiveness and joy of Jesus Christ.

AIMS OF THIS SESSION

During this session you will guide students to:

- Identify sources of temptation and how to resist temptations;
- Learn how to discern the difference between accusations from Satan and the voice of the Holy Spirit;
- Know the way to confess, renounce and receive forgiveness of sin from Christ while resisting the accusation of Satan.

KEY RESOURCES AND PREPARATION

- Read chapters 8 and 9 of *The Bondage Breaker Youth Edition.*

- Have available newspapers or magazines, newsprint or poster board, a chalkboard or flip chart, chalk or felt pens, masking tape, pencils and paper.
- Make copies of the worksheets for everyone: "Channels of Temptation" on page 101 and "Accusations and Convictions" on page 103.
- Go through all of the exercises yourself before leading the group.
- Pray that group members will ask the Holy Spirit to help them know the difference between God's voice and the accusing voice of the enemy, Satan.

Getting Started (10 minutes)

As people arrive, hand them a newspaper or magazine. Around the room have posted newsprint or poster board with these three labels: Lust of the Flesh, Lust of the Eyes, Pride of Life.

Tell people to look for pictures that could be a possible temptation in one of these areas. When they find a picture, tear it out and use masking tape to tape it up under the appropriate label.

After doing this for about five minutes, go around the room with the entire group and look at the pictures that were chosen under each label. Discuss:

How do these pictures fit the label? What temptations do they represent?

Which pictures represent evil from the outset, and which ones become evil when used in excess?

Getting Focused (10 minutes)

Read 1 John 2:15-17 in the *NASB* translation. Give everyone a copy of "Channels of Temptation."

Tell everyone that they will not have to share what they write on this worksheet with anyone but God. Give them about five minutes to complete it. Then discuss:

How did Jesus resist the temptations of Satan? What can we learn from Him?

Why do we even entertain tempting thoughts that are contrary to God's Word and will?

What is temptation?

How can we prepare ourselves for facing future temptations? Read Philippians 4:8.

Say to the group: **On the backs of your worksheets, write these questions based on Philippians 4:8.**

1. Does this thought line up with God's truth?

2. Does it suggest that I do something honorable?

3. Is it right?

4. Is it pure?

5. Will the outcome of this thought be lovely?

6. Will the result be something to admire?

7. Will it contribute to excellence in my life?

8. Is it something for which I can praise God?

Now, if you ask all of these questions to any of your thoughts and actions and the answer is no, then stop the thought or action immediately. If thoughts or actions prompt a yes to all of these, then they pass God's test for truth, honor and righteousness.

Let's test this. Everyone list one kind of thought or action that a Christian may have. Then we'll apply this test. Ask for three or four people to volunteer what action or thought they have listed, and then take the whole group through asking all of these questions to apply the test of truth. This will give some practice in doing this for the group members.

GETTING INTO THE WORD (20 MINUTES)

Have everyone read Zechariah 3:1-10. Explain what the passage means based on the explanation given in *The Bondage Breaker Youth Edition*, pp. 141-146. Be certain to cover these points and list them on a chalkboard or flip chart:

1. Satan accuses Joshua. He accuses us.
2. Accusations can make us feel dirty, guilty, hopeless and helpless.
3. The purpose of accusation is to destroy and defeat us.
4. The Lord removed Joshua's filthy garments. He washes away our sin with His blood.
5. The Holy Spirit convicts us to turn from our sins and experience the joy of forgiveness.
6. The result of the Holy Spirit's work of conviction is repentance, forgiveness and freedom from accusation and guilt.

Have everyone read 2 Corinthians 7:9,10. Divide the students into two groups. Give these instructions: **Group 1 will read Luke 22:1-6, Matthew 27:1-9.** Write texts on the board. **Group 2 will read Luke 22:33,34 and John 21:15-17.** Write texts on the board. **Both groups are to go to opposite ends of the room and prepare a pantomime of your stories. Act out the whole story and try to use everyone in your group. Remember, do not use words in your pantomime. When you perform your pantomime, the other group will try to guess what your story is about.**

After five minutes, have each group do their pantomimes with the other group trying to guess the story after the pantomime concludes. Then have this discussion:

Was Peter convicted by the Holy Spirit or accused by Satan? Give reasons for your answer.

Was Judas convicted by the Holy Spirit or accused by Satan? Give reasons.

What can we learn from Peter about how to handle guilt? What can we learn from Judas about how not to handle guilt?

GETTING REAL (10 MINUTES)

Give everyone a copy of "Accusations and Convictions." Have everyone pair up with a partner and complete their worksheets together. Help one another discern the difference between accusations and convictions.

After everyone has had about five minutes to share, discuss:

What are the characteristics of an accusation from Satan? A conviction from the Holy Spirit?

If a friend or parent voiced an accusation, what could you say in response as a Christian speaking the truth in love?

Should a Christian ever call someone dumb, stupid, geek, etc.? Why or why not?

When we accuse other Christians or feel guilty ourselves about past sins we know are forgiven, what is Satan trying to do to us?

GETTING ARMED (5 MINUTES)

Say to the group: **Share with your partners at least one statement that Satan can use to put down others, that you use at times. After both have shared their put-downs, pray this prayer: Heavenly**

Father, I ask you to show me how I have hurt others through put-downs. I ask your Holy Spirit to reveal to my mind every time I've been accused by others so I might confess and renounce them. I confess that at times I say... I renounce this put-down and ask you to forgive me, Lord. I don't want to be an accuser, like Satan. Rather, I want to follow Jesus' example and build up others. Thank You for Your forgiveness. In Jesus' name, amen.

CHANNELS OF TEMPTATION

Read 1 John 2:15-17.
Rewrite this passage in your own words. (Write a paraphrase.)

....

....

....

....

Definitions:
Lust of the flesh: temptations to fulfill our physical appetites (through food, sex, comfort, etc.).
Lust of the eyes: temptations to want everything that we can see instead of obeying God.
Pride of life: temptations to get all of the attention and glory for ourselves.

Read Matthew 4:3. Satan was tempting Jesus through the lust of the ....

Read Matthew 4:6. Satan was tempting Jesus through the lust of the ....

Read Matthew 4:8,9. Satan was tempting Jesus through the ....

On a scale of 1 to 10 (1 being least tempted and 10 being most tempted), put an X where Satan is able to tempt you the most.

Lust of the Flesh
....
1   2   3   4   5   6   7   8   9   10

Lust of the Eyes
....
1   2   3   4   5   6   7   8   9   10

Pride of Life
....
1   2   3   4   5   6   7   8   9   10

ACCUSATIONS AND CONVICTIONS

Satan accuses in order to destroy, tear down and make us feel condemned and guilty. He wants us to believe we are less than God says we are. The Holy Spirit convicts in order to help us face our sins, repent and receive forgiveness and the joy of a restored relationship with the Lord.

Write the following:

An accusation that Satan might try against you:

....

An accusation of a friend that Satan might try to get you to believe:

....

An accusation you might voice that would serve Satan's purposes:

....

An accusation against God that Satan might try to make you believe:

....

A conviction from the Holy Spirit given to you about your sin:

....

A conviction from your parents that the Holy Spirit would use to show you your sin:

....

A conviction from the Holy Spirit that would teach you about God's true nature:

....

What kind of discipline does God use to get our attention without condemning us?

....

....

WHO IS IN CONTROL
OF EVERY PART OF YOUR LIFE?

KEY VERSES

"Do not put out the Spirit's fire; do not treat prophecies with contempt. Test everything. Hold on to the good." 1 Thessalonians 5:19-21

"But there were also false prophets among the people, just as there will be false teachers among you. They will secretly introduce destructive heresies, even denying the sovereign Lord who bought them—bringing swift destruction on themselves." 2 Peter 2:1

"Dear friends, do not believe every spirit, but test the spirits to see whether they are from God, because many false prophets have gone out into the world." 1 John 4:1

Read Deuteronomy 13:5-11; Jeremiah 23.

BIBLICAL BASIS

Deuteronomy 13:5-11; Jeremiah 23; Mark 13:22; Luke 13:10-18; 22:31-34; Acts 5:1-11; Romans 12:3; 1 Corinthians 3:18,19; 5:1-13; 6:9,10; 15:33; 2 Corinthians 2:5-11; Galatians 3:5; 6:3,7; Ephesians 4:26,27; 6:10-17; 1 Thessalonians 5:19-21; 1 Timothy 4:1-3; James 3:14-16; 4:7; 1 Peter 1:13; 5:6-9; 2 Peter 2:1,10; 1 John 1:8; 4:1-6

THE BIG IDEA

Christians must discern between counterfeit spirituality and the work of the Holy Spirit through prophets, signs, wonders and teachers. A Christian cannot be owned by Satan but may allow Satan to control areas of his or her life if he or she doesn't take spiritual responsibility for that area.

AIMS OF THIS SESSION

During this session you will guide students to:
- Learn how to discern counterfeit spirituality from God's Spirit;
- Explore what self-deception and deception from others is like;
- Understand how Satan seeks to control the believer's life.

KEY RESOURCES AND PREPARATION

- Read chapters 10 and 11 in *The Bondage Breaker Youth Edition*.
- Study the explanation of how to recognize spiritual deception and the ways Satan seeks to control believers. Read all the passages in this session.

- Make copies of the worksheets for everyone: "Self-Deception" on page 109 and "Satan's Attack on Believers" on page 111.
- Have envelopes, pencils or pens and paper for everyone to write on as instructed in "Getting Armed."

GETTING STARTED (15 MINUTES)

As youth arrive, have everyone paired with a partner. Then give these instructions: **Sit face-to-face with your partner. The person with the longest hair will go first. You will have one minute to tell your partner all the good and wonderful qualities you have as God created you and as a new creation in Jesus Christ. I'll go first just to give you an example.** Have someone time you and for one minute, you give those qualities. For example, you may be a wonderful father, mother or mate; a loving person; a wonderful cook; a great tennis player; a good listener; a child of God; a saint; the salt of the earth; etc. **When I say "Go!" begin. When I say "Stop!" you'll switch and the other person will have one minute to share all those wonderful qualities from the Lord. Go!** Pause one minute. Stop and switch partners.

Have pairs form small groups of four persons. Give these instructions: **Go around the circle and each person has 30 seconds to describe their partner by all the wonderful, God-given qualities they have. Go!**

After about two minutes, give these instructions: **Starting with the smallest person in the circle and then moving to that person's right have each person in turn sit silently while everyone in the circle completes this sentence about that person: "(Name), I thank the Lord for you because** ....**." Just do one sentence, not a paragraph or long-time sharing. Just one sentence and then move around the circle until everyone has been the center of attention in this way. Go!**

GETTING FOCUSED (10 MINUTES)

Say to the group: **We are self-deceived when we believe only bad, sinful things about ourselves and not the good things that God gives us. Perhaps it was hard for you to affirm the gifts God has given you and the new creation you are becoming. That is false pride. We must claim who we are in Jesus Christ without being deceived.**

Give everyone copies of "Self-Deception." Give the group about five minutes to complete the worksheet, asking the partners to help each other. (The answers to the blanks are the following words or synonyms to these words: 1. Word; 2. sin; 3. better; 4. smarter; 5. speech; 6. consequences; 7. inherit God's kingdom; 8. bad.)

After everyone has completed the worksheets and you have given the answers, discuss:
Why do we deceive ourselves? What do we think we gain by self-deception?
What influence do others have in helping us deceive ourselves?

GETTING INTO THE WORD (20 MINUTES)

Say to the group: **Not everything that's spiritual is of the Holy Spirit. We are to put to the test everything that poses to be spiritual and genuine with the Word of God.** Read 1 Thessalonians 5:19-21. **So** we are to be aware of false prophets and teachers. What do you think distinguishes a false prophet from a true one? Discuss.

In Jeremiah 23 we read that (List these points on the board.): 1. True prophets bring people to God (verses 16,21,22); 2. A true prophet's dreams agree with God (verses 25,28); 3. A true prophet's message moves people to get right with God (verse 29); 4. The true prophet gets his message from God, not from other people (verses 30,31).

Let's read other passages that talk about Satan's counterfeits in the spiritual realm. Assign various group members to read these passages to the rest of the group: Mark 13:22; Deuteronomy 13:5-11; Galatians 3:5; 2 Peter 2:1,2,10; 1 Timothy 4:1; 1 John 4:1-6.

Discuss with the group:

How would you recognize a false teacher?

What is meant by discernment? How would you discern between God's Spirit and false spirits?

Do you believe that a demon can influence control over a Christian's life? How would that happen?

Give everyone a copy of "Satan's Attack on Believers." Divide the students into four smaller groups. Tell them to help one another complete the worksheets with various people in the groups looking up the passages and helping everyone summarize each passage.

After all the groups have completed the study, discuss:

Which form of control surprised you the most? Why?

Have you ever seen someone controlled in one of these ways? Describe what you observed?

What did you do to respond to that person?

Does Satan make us do things, or do we simply allow him control in our lives?

GETTING REAL (5 MINUTES)

Say to the group: If we don't take responsibility for our spiritual lives and growth, and take every thought captive, we will lose control to evil desires within us and to Satan. Satan cannot own a Christian, but he can influence areas of our lives if we believe one of his lies. James 4:7 says, "Submit yourselves, then to God. Resist the devil, and he will flee from you."

Find a partner. Share how you would complete these statements. (You will have one minute to both share before we go to the next statement.)

The most eye-opening thing I learned about the way Satan and his demons seek to control is

One way that I resist Satan's control is

One area of my life for which I need to put on God's armor consistently is

Getting Armed (5 minutes)

Give everyone in the group a piece of paper, pen or pencil and an envelope. Give these instructions: **Divide your paper into three parts. Label the first part of your paper: "Me." Write some of the bondages in your life that you really need freedom from in Jesus Christ. Label the second part of your paper: "Family." Write some of the bondages in your family that need to be broken by Jesus Christ. Label the third part of your paper: "Friend." Write some of the bondages that need to be broken in your friends' lives.** Tell everyone to put this into the envelope, seal it and write their names on the front. They will be given this at the next session and no one will see what they have written.

Pray this prayer in a closing circle in unison: **Lord, I confess that I am responsible at this time for giving Satan a foothold in my life, and I renounce any involvement with him in the past or present, through Jesus Christ. Amen.**

SELF-DECEPTION

The Bible tells us that there are several ways we deceive ourselves. Look up the Scriptures and then complete each sentence with what you believe is the correct word.

1. We deceive ourselves when we hear the... and don't do it (see James 1:22; 4:17).

2. We deceive ourselves when we say we have no ....(see 1 John 1:8).

3. We deceive ourselves when we think we are ....than we are (see Romans 12:3; Galatians 6:3).

4. We deceive ourselves when we think we are .... than we are (see 1 Corinthians 3:18,19).

5. We deceive ourselves when we think we are good Christians but we do not control our..........................
....(see James 1:26).

6. We deceive ourselves when we think our sin will not lead to... (see Galatians 6:7).

7. We deceive ourselves when we think people living totally in sin will.. (see 1 Corinthians 6:9,10).

8. We deceive ourselves when we think we can always hang out with... people and not be influenced by them (see 1 Corinthians 15:33).

Satan's Attack on Believers

Read each of the following passages, and summarize with just a phrase or a few words how Satan attacks people and seeks to control believers.

Luke 13:10-18

Luke 22:31-34

Acts 5:1-11

1 Corinthians 5:1-13

2 Corinthians 2:5-11

Ephesians 4:26,27

Ephesians 6:10-17

1 Timothy 4:1-3

James 3:14-16

1 Peter 5:6-9

BEING SET FREE AND LIVING FREE

KEY VERSES

"It is for freedom that Christ has set us free. Stand firm, then, and do not let yourselves be burdened again by a yoke of slavery." Galatians 5:1

BIBLICAL BASIS

John 8:32,36; Romans 6:18; 8:1,2; Galatians 5:1; Revelation 1:5

THE BIG IDEA

God's Word is a specific tool leading us through steps toward freedom in Christ Jesus from every bondage.

AIMS OF THIS SESSION

During this session you will guide students to:
- Go through specific, biblical steps to be set free of bondages;
- Learn what they can do after the course to walk in Christ's freedom.

KEY RESOURCES AND PREPARATION

- Carefully read chapter 12 of *The Bondage Breaker Youth Edition* and go through the steps yourself (preferably with a prayer partner) before you lead the group in this session.
- Make 3x5-inch cards with the entire freedom verse written on it. Do not just quote the passage reference. The group members need the entire verse. If there are many in your group, you may want to make a master copy of each verse and run the other cards through a copy machine. Here are the verses: John 8:32; John 8:36; Romans 6:18; Romans 8:1,2; Galatians 5:1; Revelation 1:5.
- Make copies of the worksheets "Steps to Freedom in Christ" on pages 117-163 for everyone in the group.
- Have envelopes from Session 12, pencils and paper for everyone. Also have tissues for tears that may be shed in this final session.

GETTING STARTED (5 MINUTES)

This session will be different than the previous sessions as it will give each person in the group an opportunity to deal with the bondages in his or her life at a deeper level than previous sessions. As people come into the room, give them the envelopes that have their names on them from the previous session. If someone comes that was not there for the previous session, reassure them that they will be able to catch up quickly when the envelopes are used.

As people come in, also hand them a 3x5-inch card with one of the freedom verses written on it. Give these instructions: **On your card is a verse about the freedom Christ has given us as believers. Go around to everyone in the group and share your verse with them until everyone else has heard your verse and, of course, you have heard theirs.** Give the group about two minutes to do this. **Now find a partner, perhaps someone you have had as a partner in previous sessions. If you do not have an envelope, get with a partner that doesn't have one either, if there is another. I will partner with anyone left who needs a partner.**

Getting Focused and into the Word (45 minutes)

Instead of breaking up the rest of this session into individual teaching segments, we shall follow the steps listed in chapter 12 of *The Bondage Breaker Youth Edition*.

To prepare for leading these steps be certain that you have:
• Gone through them prior to the session for yourself.
• Become familiar enough with each that you can summarize and paraphrase its teaching in your own words.

Have students sit with their partners. Give everyone a copy of "Steps to Freedom in Christ" and a pencil or pen.

Ask everyone to take a minute and read through the paper in their envelopes written during Session 12. If a person does not have an envelope, ask them to list on a blank piece of paper any bondage in their lives, their families, or with their friends, from which they would like to be set free by Christ. As you walk the pairs through these steps, explain that the partners only have to share with one another what they feel comfortable sharing. If they want their partner to pray with them, that is what the partner is there for, but if they want to pray privately, they may do so.

Give a brief summary of each step as you have become familiar with the material in chapter 12 of *The Bondage Breaker Youth Edition*. Also tell the group members that if a particular step does not apply to them, then to spend that time in prayer for others in the group.

Getting Real and Armed (5 minutes)

Tell the group: **Daily victory and walking in spiritual maturity and freedom requires you to:**
1. **Strengthen your freedom with fellowship.**
2. **Strengthen your freedom by studying God's Word.**
3. **Strengthen your freedom through daily prayer.**
4. **Strengthen your freedom by taking every thought captive.**
5. **Strengthen your freedom by understanding who you are in Christ.**
6. **Strengthen your freedom through sharing your faith.**

Take a final moment to pray for your partner. Repeat this prayer after me. Lord God, empower (name) through your Holy Spirit to be strengthened each day in fellowship, the Word, prayer, taking every thought captive, understanding himself or herself as a new creation in Jesus Christ and in sharing their faith in Christ. In Jesus' name, amen.

In a closing circle, ask each person who may wish to, to share one way God has touched their life in this course.

Finally, invite the group to pray the following prayer by repeating it after you: **Dear heavenly Father, I honor You as my Lord. I know that You are always present with me. You are the only all-powerful, all-knowing God. You are kind and loving in all Your ways. I love You and thank You that I am united with Christ and spiritually alive in Him. I choose not to love the world, and I put to death all my sinful desires. I thank You for the life that I now have in Christ, and I ask You to fill me and guide me with Your Holy Spirit so I can live my life free from sin. I declare my dependence upon You, and I take my stand against Satan and all his lying ways. I choose to believe the truth, and I refuse to be discouraged. You are the God of all hope, and I am confident that You will meet my needs as I seek to live according to Your Word. I am confident that I can live a responsible life through Christ who strengthens me. I now take a stand against Satan and command him and all his evil spirits to depart from me. I put on the full armor of God. I submit my body as a living sacrifice and renew my mind by the living Word of God in order that I may prove that the will of God is good, acceptable and perfect. I ask these things in the precious name of my Lord and Savior, Jesus Christ, amen.**

STEPS TO FREEDOM IN CHRIST

Spiritual freedom is meant for every Christian, young or old. Freedom in Christ is having the desire and power to do God's will. It is *knowing* God's truth, *believing* God's truth and *living* according to God's truth. It is knowing the joy of our salvation through a life of experiencing Jesus' love, for God, Himself, and for other people. Being free in Christ means being released from the chains of the sins of our past, problems of the present and fears of the future. It is a walk in the Spirit, experiencing the fruit of the Spirit. It is not a life of perfection, but *progress*! All these qualities may not be yours now, but they are meant for everyone who is in Christ.

If you have already received Christ as your Savior, He has set you free through His victory over sin and death on the cross. If freedom is not a constant reality for you, it may be because you have not understood how Christ can help you deal with the pain of your past or problems of your present life. It is *your* responsibility as one who knows Christ to do whatever is needed to have and maintain a right relationship with God. Your eternal life is not at stake; you are safe and secure in Christ. But you will not experience all that Christ has for you if you do not understand who you are in Christ and do not live according to that truth.

We've got great news for you! You may be young but you are not a helpless victim caught between two nearly equal but opposite heavenly superpowers, God and Satan. Satan is a deceiver. Only God is all-powerful, always present and all-knowing. Sometimes sin and the presence of evil may seem more real than the presence of God, but that's part of Satan's tricky lie. Satan is a defeated enemy, and we are in Christ, the Victor. Understanding who God is and who we are in Christ are the two most important factors in determining our daily victory over sin and Satan. False beliefs about God, not understanding who we are as children of God and making Satan out to be as powerful and present as God are the greatest causes of spiritual defeat.

The battle is for your mind. During this session, you may experience nagging thoughts like, *This isn't going to work*, or *God doesn't love me*. Those thoughts are lies, implanted in your mind by deceiving spirits. If you believe them, you will really struggle working though these steps. Those opposing thoughts can control you only if you believe them.

If you are working though these steps by yourself, don't pay attention to any lying or threatening thoughts in your mind. If you're working through them with a trusted friend, youth pastor, parent or counselor (which we strongly recommend), then share any thoughts that you are having that are in opposition to what you are trying to do. As soon as you uncover the lie and choose to believe the truth, the power of Satan is broken.

You must cooperate with the person who is trying to help you. Do this by sharing what is going on inside your mind. Also, if you experience any physical discomfort (e.g. headache, nausea, tightness in the throat, etc.), don't be alarmed. Just tell the person you are with so that he/she can pray for you.

As believers in Christ, we can pray with authority to stop any interference by Satan. Here is a prayer and declaration to get you started. Read them (and all prayers and declarations in these steps) aloud.

Prayer:

Dear heavenly Father, we know that You are always here in this room and present in our lives. You are the only all-knowing, all-powerful, ever-present God. We des-

perately need You, because without Jesus we can do nothing. We believe the Bible because it tells us what is really true. We refuse to believe the lies of Satan. We stand in the truth that all authority in heaven and on earth has been given to the resurrected Christ. Because we are in Christ, we share His authority in order to make followers of Jesus and set captives free. We ask You to protect our thoughts and minds, fill us with Your Holy Spirit, and lead us into all truth. Please reveal to our minds everything that You want to deal with today. We ask for and trust in Your wisdom. We pray for Your complete protection over us. In Jesus' name, amen.

Declaration:

In the name and the authority of the Lord Jesus Christ, we command Satan and all evil spirits to let go of (name) in order that (name) can be free to know and choose to do the will of God. As children of God, seated with Christ in the heavenlies, we agree that every enemy of the Lord Jesus Christ be bound and gagged to silence in (name). We say to Satan and all of his evil workers that you cannot inflict any pain or in any way stop or hinder God's will from being done today in (name's) life.

Preparation
Before you start these "Steps to Freedom," go over the events of your life so that you understand the areas that might need to be dealt with. If you have the *Confidential Spiritual Inventory*, it would be helpful to complete it now.

Family History:
❑ Religious background of parents and grandparents
❑ Your home life from childhood to the present
❑ Any history of physical or emotional problems in the family
❑ Adoption, foster care, guardians

Personal History:
❑ Spiritual journey—Do you know if you are saved? If yes, how do you know you are saved? When did that happen?
❑ Eating habits—Do you make yourself vomit, take laxatives or starve yourself to lose weight? Do you binge or eat uncontrollably?
• Free Time
❑ How many hours of TV do you watch a day?
❑ What are your favorite TV shows?
❑ How much time do you spend playing video/computer games each day?
❑ How much time do you spend listening to music a day?
❑ What kind of music do you listen to?

❑ How much time do you spend reading each day?
❑ What do you spend most of your time reading?
❑ Do you smoke? ❑ Chew tobacco? ❑ Drink alcohol?
❑ Do you use street drugs? If so, what kind?...
❑ Prescription drugs? What for?...
❑ Have you ever run away from home?
❑ Do you have trouble sleeping too little or too much?
❑ Do you have frequent or recurring nightmares?
❑ Were you ever raped or abused sexually, physically, verbally or emotionally?
❑ Do you suffer from distracting thoughts while in church, prayer or Bible study?

• Physical life (Check those that apply to you.)

❑ Frequent headaches/migraines
❑ Constant tiredness
❑ Dizziness
❑ Stomach problems

❑ Memory problems
❑ Fainting spells
❑ Shortness of breath
❑ Allergies

• Thought life (Check those that apply to you.)

❑ Daydreaming/fantasizing
❑ Thoughts of inferiority
❑ Racing or rushing thoughts
❑ Perfectionism
❑ Self-hateful thoughts
❑ Thoughts of suicide

❑ Doubts about salvation or God's love
❑ Worry
❑ Insecurity
❑ Lust
❑ Thoughts of inadequacy

• Emotional life (Check those that apply to you.)

❑ Feelings of frustration
❑ Anger
❑ Anxiety
❑ Loneliness
❑ Depression
❑ Guilt
❑ Fear of confusion
❑ Worthlessness
❑ Bitterness

❑ Fear of death
❑ Fear of losing your mind
❑ Fear of committing suicide
❑ Fear of terminal illness
❑ Fear of failure
❑ Fear of going to hell
❑ Fear of being homosexual
❑ Fear of parents divorcing
❑ Fear of..

Now you are ready to start. Here are seven steps to help you be free from your past. You will cover the areas where Satan most often takes advantage of us and where strongholds have been built. Christ purchased your victory when He shed His blood for you on the cross. You will experience your freedom when you make the choice to believe, confess, forgive, renounce and forsake. No one can do that for you. The battle for your mind can only be won as you *personally* choose truth.

As you go through these *Steps to Freedom in Christ*, remember that Satan cannot read your mind, thus he won't obey your thoughts. Only God knows what you are thinking. As you go through each step, it is important that you submit to God inwardly and resist the devil by reading aloud each prayer—verbally renouncing, forgiving, confessing, etc.

You are going to be taking a thorough look at your life in order to get radically right with God. If you find that you have another kind of problem (not covered in these steps) which is negatively affecting your

life, you will have lost nothing. If you are open and honest during this time, you will greatly benefit anyway by becoming right with God and close to Him again.

May the Lord greatly touch your life during this time. He will give you the strength to persevere. It is essential that you work through all seven steps, so don't allow yourself to become discouraged and give up. Remember, the freedom that Christ purchased for all believers on the cross is meant for *you!*

Step 1: Counterfeit vs. Real

The first step toward experiencing your freedom in Christ is to renounce (to reject and turn your back on all past, present and future involvement with) any participation in Satan-inspired occult practices, things done in secret and non-Christian religions. You must renounce any activity and group which denies Jesus Christ, offers direction through any source other than the absolute authority of the written Word of God, or requires secret initiations, ceremonies, promises or pacts (covenants). Begin with the following prayer:

> **Dear heavenly Father, I ask You to reveal to me anything that I have done or that someone has done to me that is spiritually wrong. Reveal to my mind any and all involvement I have knowingly or unknowingly had with cult or occult practices and/or false teachers. I want to experience Your freedom and do only Your will. I ask this in Jesus' name, amen.**

Even if you took part in something as a game or as a joke, you need to renounce it. We need to realize that Satan will try and take advantage of anything he can in our lives. Even if you were just standing by and watching others do it, you need to renounce it. Even if you did it just once and had no idea it was evil, still you need to renounce it. You want to make sure to remove any and every possible foothold of Satan in your life.

Non-Christian Spiritual Check List
(Check all those that apply to you.)

❑ Out of body experience
   (astral projection)
❑ Ouija board
❑ Bloody Mary
❑ Light as a feather
   (or other occult games)
❑ Christian Science
❑ Table lifting or body lifting
❑ Magic Eight Ball
❑ Using spells or curses
❑ Attempting to control others by
   putting thoughts in their heads
❑ Automatic writing
❑ Spirit guides
❑ Fortune-telling

❑ Mormonism

❑ Jehovah Witness
❑ New Age
❑ New Age Medicine

❑ Masons
❑ Science of the Mind
❑ Science of Creative Intelligence
❑ The Way International
❑ Unification Church (Moonies)

❑ The Forum (EST)
❑ Church of the Living Word
❑ Children of God (Children of Love)

❑ Tarot cards
❑ Palm reading
❑ Astrology/horoscopes
❑ Hypnosis
❑ Seances
❑ Black or white magic
❑ Dungeons and Dragons (or other fantasy role-playing games)
❑ Video or computer games involving occult powers or cruel violence
❑ Blood pacts or cutting yourself on purpose
❑ Objects of worship/crystals/ good luck charms
❑ Sexual spirits
❑ Martial Arts (involving Eastern mysticism meditation or devotion to sensei
❑ Buddhism (including Zen)
❑ Rosicrucianism
❑ Hinduism

❑ Worldwide Church of God (Armstrong)
❑ Scientology
❑ Unitarianism
❑ Roy Masters
❑ Silva Mind Control
❑ Transcendental Meditation (TM)
❑ Yoga
❑ Hare Krishna
❑ Bahaism
❑ Native American spirit worship
❑ Idols of rock stars, actors/actresses, sports heroes, etc.
❑ Islam
❑ Black Muslim

(NOTE: This is not a complete list. If you have any doubts about an activity not included here, renounce your involvement in it. If it has come to mind here, trust that the Lord wants you to renounce it.)

Anti-Christian movies

....

....

....

....

....

Anti-Christian music

....

....

....

....

....

Anti-Christian TV shows or video games

....

....

....

....

Anti-Christian books, magazines and comics

....

....

....

....

❑ Have you ever heard or seen a spiritual being in your room?

❑ Have you had an imaginary friend that talked to you?

❑ Have you ever heard voices in your head or had repeating, nagging thoughts like, "I'm dumb," "I'm ugly," "Nobody loves me," "I can't do anything right," etc., like there was a conversation going on in your head? Explain.

❑ Have you or anyone in your family ever consulted a medium, spiritist or channeler? If yes, who?

❑ What other spiritual experiences have you had that would be considered out of the ordinary? (Telepathy, speaking in a trance, known something supernaturally, contact with aliens, etc.)

❑ Have you ever been involved in satanic worship of any kind or attended a concert in which Satan was the focus?

Once you have completed that checklist, confess and renounce each item you were involved in by praying aloud the following prayer. (Repeat the prayer separately for each item on your list.)

Lord, I confess that I have participated in..

I thank You for Your forgiveness and I renounce any and all involvement with..........................

....

If you have been involved in any satanic rituals or heavy occult activity (or you suspect it because of blocked memories, severe and recurring nightmares or sexual bondage), you need to say aloud the following special renunciations and affirmations.

Read across the page, renouncing the first item in the column under "Domain of Darkness" and then affirming the first truth in the column under "Kingdom of Light." Continue down this page and the next in that manner.

In addition to the lists below, all satanic rituals, covenants (promises) and assignments must be *specifically* renounced as the Lord brings them to your mind. Some people who have been subjected to satanic Ritual Abuse (SRA) develop multiple personalities (alters) in order to cope with their pain. In this case, you need someone who understands spiritual conflict to help walk you through this. You can continue to walk through these *Steps to Freedom in Christ* in order to resolve all that you are aware of. It is important that you remove any demonic strongholds in your life first. Eventually, every alter personality (if this is your situation) must be identified and guided into resolving the issues that caused its formation. Then, all true alters can agree to come together in Christ.

Domain of Darkness

1. I renounce ever signing my name to Satan or having my name signed over to Satan by someone else.
2. I renounce any ceremony where I was wed to Satan.
3. I renounce any and all covenants, agreement, or promises that I made with Satan.
4. I renounce all satanic assignments

Kingdom of Light

1. I announce that my name is now written in the Lamb's Book of Life.
2. I announce that I am the Bride of Christ.
3. I announce that I have made a new covenant with Jesus Christ alone.
4. I announce and commit myself

Being Set Free and Living Free

for my life, including duties, marriage and children.

5. I renounce all spirit guides assigned to me.
6. I renounce ever giving of my blood in the service of Satan.
7. I renounce ever eating flesh or drinking blood in satanic worship.

8. I renounce all guardians and satanic parents that were assigned to me.

9. I renounce any baptism whereby I am identified with Satan.
10. I renounce every sacrifice made on my behalf by which Satan may claim ownership of me.

to know and do only the will of God and I accept only His guiance for my life.

5. I announce and accept only the leading of the Holy Spirit.
6. I trust only in the shed blood of Lord Jesus Christ.
7. By faith I eat only the flesh and drink only the blood of the Lord Jesus in Holy Communion.

8. I announce that God is my heavenly Father and the Holy Spirit is my guardian by whom I am sealed.

9. I announce that I have been baptized into Christ Jesus and my identity is now in Him.
10. I announce that only the sacrifice of Christ has any claim on me. I belong to Him. I have been purchased by the blood of the Lamb.

Step 2: Deception vs. Truth

God's Word is true, and we need to accept the truth deep in our hearts (see Psalm 51:6). When David lived a lie, he really suffered. When he finally found freedom by admitting that he'd sinned, he wrote, "Blessed is the man...in whose spirit is no deceit" (see Psalm 32:2). We must stop lying to ourselves and to each other and speak the truth in love (see Ephesians 4:15,25). A mentally healthy young person can face the truth, live in a real world and not let any fear control him or her. We are told in Scripture that God is the only One we should fear. This means that we hold Him in highest respect and have a great awe of His power, majesty and holiness.

Start this important step by praying the following prayer aloud. Don't let any opposing thoughts such as, *This isn't going to work, This is a waste of time* or *I wish I could believe this but I just can't* keep you from praying and choosing the truth. Belief is a choice. If you choose to believe what you feel, then Satan, the "father of lies" will keep you in bondage. We must choose to believe what God says, regardless of what our feelings might say. Even if you have a hard time doing it, pray the following prayer.

Dear heavenly Father, I know that You want me to face the truth and that I must be honest with You. I know that choosing to believe the truth will set me free. I have been deceived by Satan, the father of lies, and I have deceived myself as well. I thought I could hide from You, but You see everything and still love me. I pray in the name of the Lord Jesus Christ asking You to rebuke all of Satan's demons

through Your righteous Son, Jesus Christ, who shed His blood and rose from the dead for me.

I have trusted in Jesus alone to save me, and so I am Your child. Therefore, by the authority of the Lord Jesus Christ, I command all evil spirits to leave my presence. I ask the Holy Spirit to lead me into all truth. I ask You, Father, to look deep inside me and know my heart. Show me if there is anything in me that I am trying to hide, because I want to be free. In Jesus' name, amen.

It is important that you now take some time to let God reveal any of Satan's evil tricks that he's used against you in your life. It is important to know that, in addition to false teachers and deceiving spirits, you can fool yourself. Now that you are alive in Christ and forgiven, you don't need to live a lie or defend yourself like you used to. Christ is now your truth and defense.

Ways you can deceive yourself:
❏ Hearing God's Word but not doing it (see James 1:22; 4:17)
❏ Saying, "I have no sin" (see 1 John 1:8)
❏ Thinking I am something I'm really not (see Galatians 6:3)
❏ Thinking I am wise in the things of the world (see 1 Corinthians 3:18,19)
❏ Thinking I will not reap what I sow (see Galatians 6:7)
❏ Thinking that ungodly people who live lives of sin will share in God's kingdom (see 1 Corinthians 6:9,10)
❏ Thinking I can hang out with bad people and they won't have any bad influence on me (see 1 Corinthians 15:33)
❏ Thinking I can be a good Christian and still hurt others by what I say (see James 1:26)
Use the following prayer of confession for each item above that you have believed. Pray through each item separately.

Lord, I confess that I have deceived myself by... **. I thank You for Your forgiveness and commit myself to believing Your truth.**

Wrong ways of defending yourself:
❏ Refusing to face the bad things that have happened to me (denial of reality)
❏ Escape from the real world by daydreaming, TV, movies, computer or video games, music, etc. (fantasy)
❏ Withdraw from people to avoid rejection (emotional insulation)
❏ Reverting (going back) to a less threatening time of life (regression)
❏ Taking out frustrations on others (displaced anger)
❏ Blaming others for your problems (projection)
❏ Making excuses for poor behavior (rationalization)
Use the confession on the following page for each item above that you have participated in. Pray through each item separately.

Lord, I confess that I have defended myself wrongly by

....**. I thank You for Your forgiveness**

and commit myself to trusting in You to defend and protect me.

Choosing the truth may be difficult if you have been living a lie and have been deceived for some time. The Christian needs only one defense, Jesus. Knowing that you are completely forgiven and accepted as God's child sets you free to face reality and declare your total dependence upon Him.

Faith is the biblical response to the truth, and believing the truth is a choice we can all make. If you say, "I want to believe God, but I just can't," you are being deceived. Of course you can believe God, because what God says is always true.

Faith is something you decide to do, whether or not you feel like doing it. Believing the truth doesn't make it true, however. *It's true, therefore we believe it.*

The New Age movement twists the truth by saying we create reality through what we believe. We can't create reality with our minds. We *face* reality with our minds.

Simply "having faith" is not the key issue here. It's what or whom you believe in that makes the difference. You see, everybody believes in something and everybody lives according to what he or she believes. The question is: Is the object of your faith trustworthy? If what you believe is not true, then how you live will not be right.

For centuries, Christians have known that it is important to tell others what they believe. Read aloud the following "Statement of Truth," thinking about the words as you read them. Read it every day for several weeks. This will help you renew your mind and will replace any lies you have believed with the truth.

Statement of Truth:

1. **I believe that there is only one true and living God** (see Exodus 20:2,3) **who is the Father, Son and Holy Spirit. He is worthy of all honor, praise and glory. I believe that He made all things and holds all things together** (see Colossians 1:16,17).

2. **I recognize Jesus Christ as the Messiah, the Word who became flesh and lived with us** (see John 1:1,14). **I believe that He came to destroy the works of the devil** (see 1 John 3:8).

3. **I believe that God showed how much He loved me by having Jesus die for me, even though I was sinful** (see Romans 5:8). **I believe that God rescued me from the dark power of Satan and brought me into the kingdom of His Son, who forgives my sins and sets me free** (see Colossians 1:13,14).

4. **I believe I am spiritually strong because Jesus is my strength. I have authority to stand against Satan because I am God's child** (see 1 John 3:1-3). **I believe that I was saved by the grace of God through faith, that it was a gift and not the result of any works of mine** (see Ephesians 2:8,9).

5. **I choose to be strong in the Lord and in the strength of His might** (see Ephesians 6:10). **I put no confidence in the flesh** (see Philippians 3:3) **because my weapons of spiritual battle are not of the flesh, but are powerful through God, for the tearing down of Satan's strongholds** (see 2 Corinthians 10:4). **I put on the whole armor of God** (see Ephesians 6:10-20), **and I resolve to stand firm in my faith and resist the evil one** (see 1 Peter 5:8,9).

6. **I believe that apart from Christ I can do nothing** (see John 15:5) **yet I can do all things**

through Him who strengthens me (see Philippians 4:13). **Therefore, I choose to rely totally on Christ. I choose to abide in Christ in order to bear much fruit and glorify the Lord** (see John 15:8). **I announce to Satan that Jesus is my Lord** (see 1 Corinthians 12:3), **and I reject any counterfeit gifts or works of Satan in my life.**

7. **I believe that the truth will set me free** (see John 8:32). **I stand against Satan's lies by taking every thought captive in obedience to Christ** (see 2 Corinthians 10:5). **I believe that the Bible is the only reliable guide for my life** (see 2 Timothy 3:15,16). **I choose to speak the truth in love** (see Ephesians 4:15).

8. **I choose to present my body as an instrument of righteousness, a living and holy sacrifice and to renew my mind with God's Word** (see Romans 6:13; 12:1,2). **I put off the old self with its evil practices and put on the new self** (see Colossians 3:9,10). **I am a new creation in Christ** (see 2 Corinthians 5:17).

9. **I ask my heavenly Father to fill me with His Holy Spirit** (see Ephesians 5:18), **so that He can guide me into all truth** (see John 16:13). **He will give me strength to live above sin and not carry out the desires of my flesh. I crucify the flesh and choose to be led by and obey the Holy Spirit** (see Galatians 5:16,24).

10. **I renounce all selfish goals and choose the greatest goal of love** (see 1 Timothy 1:5). **I choose to obey the two greatest commandments to love the Lord my God with all my heart, soul, and mind and love my neighbor as myself** (see Matthew 22:37-39).

11. **I believe that Jesus has all authority in heaven and on earth** (see Matthew 28:18) **and that He rules over everything** (see Colossians 2:10). **I believe that Satan and his demons have been defeated by Christ and are subject to me since I am a member of Christ's Body** (see Ephesians 1:19-20; 2:6). **So, I obey the command to submit to God and to resist the devil** (see James 4:7) **and I command Satan, by the authority of the Lord Jesus Christ, to leave my presence.**

Step 3: Bitterness vs. Forgiveness

If you have not forgiven others, you've become a wide-open target for Satan to shoot at. God commands us to forgive others as we have been forgiven (see Ephesians 4:32). You need to obey this command so that Satan can't take advantage of you (see 2 Corinthians 2:11).

Christians are to forgive others and show them mercy because our heavenly Father has been merciful to us. Ask God to bring to your mind the names of those people you need to forgive by praying the following prayer aloud. (Remember to let this prayer come from your heart as well as your mouth!)

Dear heavenly Father, I thank You for Your great kindness and patience, I know that Your kindness has led me to turn from my sins (see Romans 2:4). **I know that I have not been completely kind, patient and loving toward those who have hurt me. I have had bad thoughts and feelings toward them. I ask You now to bring to the surface all my painful memories so that I can choose to forgive these people from my heart. I ask You, too, to bring to my mind all the people that I need to forgive** (see

Matthew 18:35). **I pray this in the precious name of Jesus, who has forgiven me and who will heal me from my hurts, amen.**

On a sheet of paper, make a list of the names of people that come to your mind. At this point, don't question whether you need to forgive them or not. If a name comes to your mind, write it.

After God's Spirit finishes the list, write "me" at the bottom. Forgiving yourself means accepting God's cleansing and forgiveness. Also write "thoughts against God." It is very common to harbor angry thoughts toward God, though we don't actually need to forgive Him because He is perfect.

Sometimes, however, we expect or even demand that God act in a certain way in our lives. When He doesn't do what we want in the way we want, we can get angry. Those feelings can become a wall between us and God, and so we must let them go.

Before you begin working through the process of forgiving the people on your list, stop and consider what real forgiveness is and what it is *not*.

Forgiveness is not forgetting. People who want to be able to forget all their pain before they get around to forgiving someone, usually find they cannot. God commands us to forgive *now*. Confusion sometimes arises because Scripture says that God "will remember no more our sins" (see Hebrews 10:17). But God knows everything and can't "forget" as if He had no memory of our sin. God promises that He will never use your past against you (see Psalm 103:10). The key issue is this: You may not be able to forget your past, but you can be free from it by forgiving others. When we bring up the past and use it against others, we are showing that we have not yet forgiven them (see Mark 11:25).

Forgiveness is a choice, a decision of the will. Since God requires us to forgive, it is something we can do. Forgiveness seems hard because it pulls against our sense of what is right and fair. We naturally want revenge for the things we have suffered. But we are told by God never to take our own revenge (see Romans 12:19).

You might be thinking, *Why should I let them off the hook?* That is exactly the problem! As long as you do not forgive, you are still hooked to those who hurt you! You are still chained to your past. By forgiving, you let them off your hook, but they are not off God's hook. We must trust Him to deal with the other person justly, fairly and mercifully, something we cannot do.

You say, "But you don't know how much this person hurt me." Don't you see? Until you let go of your hate and anger, they are still hurting you! How do you finally stop the pain? By forgiving someone. You forgive for your sake, so that you can be free. Forgiveness is mainly an issue of obedience between you and God. God wants you to be free; this is the only way.

Forgiveness is agreeing to live with the consequences of another person's sin. Forgiveness costs you something. You choose to pay the price for the evil you forgive. But you are going to live with the consequences whether you want to or not. Your only choice is whether you will do so in the bondage of bitterness or in the freedom of forgiveness.

Of course, Jesus took the eternal consequences of all sin upon Himself. God "made Him who had no sin to be sin for us, so that in him we might become the righteousness of God" (2 Corinthians 5:21). We need, however, to accept the temporary consequences of what was done for us. But no one truly forgives without suffering the pain of another's sin.

That can seem unfair and we wonder, where is the justice? It is found at the Cross which makes forgiveness legally and morally right. Jesus prayed as those who crucified Him mocked and jeered Him, "Father, forgive them for they do not know what they are doing" (Luke 23:34).

How do you forgive from your heart? You allow God to bring to the surface the mental agony, emo-

tional pain and feelings of hurt toward those who hurt you. If your forgiveness doesn't bring out or reach down to the emotional core of your life, it will be incomplete. Too often we try to bury the pain deep down inside us, making it hard to get in touch with how we really feel. Though we may not know how to, or even want to bring our feelings to the surface, God does. Let God bring the pain to the surface so that He can deal with it. This is where God's gentle healing process begins.

Forgiveness is deciding not to use that offense against the person who has hurt you. It is common for us to remember a past, hurtful event and find the anger and hate we felt returning. We can be tempted to bring up the issue with the one who hurt us in order to make them feel bad. But we must choose to take that thought of revenge captive to the obedience of Christ, and choose to maintain forgiveness.

This doesn't mean that you must continue to put up with the future sins of others. God does not tolerate sin and neither should you. Nor should you put yourself in the position of being continually abused and hurt by the sins of others. You need to take a stand against sin while continuing to forgive those who hurt you.

Don't wait to forgive until you feel like forgiving. You will never get there. Your emotions will begin to heal once you have obeyed God's command to forgive. Satan will have lost his power over you in that area and God's healing touch will take over. For now, it is freedom that will be gained, not necessarily a feeling.

As you pray, God may bring to mind painful memories that you had totally forgotten. Let Him do this, even if it hurts. God wants you to be free; forgiving these people is the only way. Don't try to excuse the offender's behavior, even if it is someone close to you.

Remember that forgiveness is dealing with your own pain and leaving the other person to deal with God. Good feelings will follow in time. Freeing yourself from the past is the critical issue right now.

Don't say, "Lord, please help me to forgive." He is already helping you and will be with you all the way through the process. Don't say, "Lord, I want to forgive" because that bypasses the hard choice we have to make. Say, "Lord, I forgive."

As you move down your list, stay with each individual until you are sure you have dealt with all the remembered pain, everything they did that hurt you, and how they made you feel (rejected, unloved, unworthy, dirty, etc.).

It's time to begin. For each person on your list, pray aloud:

Lord, I forgive (name the person) **for** (say what they did to hurt you) **even though it made me feel** (share the painful memories or feelings)**.**

Once you have dealt with every offense that has come to your mind and you have honestly expressed how that person hurt you, then conclude forgiving him/her by praying:

Lord, I choose not to hold any of these things against (name) **any longer. I thank You for setting me free from the bondage of my bitterness toward him (or her). I choose now to ask You to bless** (name). **In Jesus' name, amen.**

Step 4: Rebellion vs. Submission

We live in rebellious times. Often young people today don't respect people in the positions of the authority that God has placed over them. They have a lot of problems with living in submission to them.

You can easily be deceived into thinking that those in authority over you are robbing you of your freedom. In reality, however, God has placed them there for your protection.

Rebelling against God and His authorities is serious business. It gives Satan an opportunity to attack you. Submission is the only solution. God requires more of you, however, than just the outward appearance of submission. He wants you to sincerely submit to your authorities (especially parents) from the heart.

When you submit, your commanding general, the Lord Jesus Christ, is telling you to "Get into ranks and follow Me!" He promises that He will not lead you into temptation, but will deliver you from evil (see Matthew 6:13).

The Bible makes it clear that we have two responsibilities toward those in authority over us: to pray for them and submit to them. Pray the following prayer aloud from your heart.

> **Dear heavenly Father, You have said in the Bible that rebellion is the same thing as witchcraft, and being self-willed is like serving false gods. I know that I have disobeyed and rebelled in my heart against You and those You have placed in authority over me. I thank You for Your forgiveness for my rebellion. By the shed blood of the Lord Jesus Christ, I pray that all doors that I opened to evil spirits through my rebellion would now be closed. I pray that You will show me all the ways I have been rebellious. I choose to adopt a submissive spirit and servant's heart. In Jesus' precious name I pray, amen.**

Being under authority is an act of faith! By submitting, you are trusting God to work through His lines of authority.

There may be times when parents, teachers, etc. abuse their authority and break the laws which are ordained by God for the protection of innocent people. In those cases, you need to seek help from a higher authority for your protection. The laws in your state may require that such abuse be reported to the police or other protective agency.

If there is continuing abuse (physical, mental, emotional or sexual) at home, further counseling help may be needed to change this situation.

If authorities abuse their position by clearly asking you to break God's law or compromise your commitment to Him, you need to obey God rather than man.

We are all told to submit to one another in the fear of Christ (see Ephesians 5:21). In addition, however, God uses specific lines of authority to protect us and give order to our daily lives.

❑ Civil government—including traffic laws, drinking laws, etc. (see Romans 13:1-7; 1 Timothy 2:1-4; 1 Peter 2:13-17)

❑ Parents (see Ephesians 6:1-3)

❑ Teachers, coaches, and school officials (see Romans 13:1-4)

❑ Your boss (see 1 Peter 2:18-21)
❑ Husband (see Ephesians 5:22-24)
❑ Church leaders—pastor, youth pastor, Sunday school teacher (see Hebrews 13:17)
❑ God, Himself (see Daniel 9:5,9)

Examine each of the six areas of authority listed above and ask the Lord to forgive you for those times you have not respected their position or been submissive to them, by praying:

Lord, I agree with You that I have been rebellious toward

.... **. Please forgive me for this**

rebellion. I choose to be submissive and obedient to Your Word. In Jesus' name,

amen.

Step 5: Pride vs. Humility

Pride is a killer. Pride says, "I can do it! I can get myself out of this mess without God or anyone else's help." Oh no we can't! We absolutely need God, and we desperately need each other. Paul wrote, "We who worship by the Spirit of God, who glory in Christ Jesus, and who put no confidence in the flesh" (Philippians 3:3).

Humility is confidence properly placed in God. We are to be "strong in the Lord and in his mighty power" (Ephesians 6:10). James 4:6-10 and 1 Peter 5:1-10 tell us that spiritual problems will follow when we are proud. Use the following prayer to express your commitment to live humbly before God.

Dear heavenly Father, You have said that pride goes before destruction and an arro-
gant spirit before stumbling (see Proverbs 16:18). **I confess that I have been thinking**
mainly of myself and not of others. I have not denied myself, picked up my cross
daily and followed You (see Matthew 16:24). **In so doing, I have given ground to the**
enemy in my life. I have believed that I could be successful by living according to
my own power and resources. I now confess that I have sinned against You by plac-
ing my will before Yours and by centering my life around myself instead of You. I
renounce my pride and my selfishness and by so doing close any doors I opened in
my life or physical body to the enemies of the Lord Jesus Christ. I ask You to fill me
with the Holy Spirit so I can do Your will. I give my heart to You and stand against
all the ways that Satan attacks me. I ask You to show me how to live for others. I
now choose to make others more important than myself and to make You the most
important of all in my life (see Matthew 6:33; Romans 12:10). **Please show me specifi-**

cally now the ways in which I have lived pridefully. I ask this in the name of my Lord Jesus Christ, amen.

Having made that commitment in prayer, now allow God to show you any specific areas of your life where you have been prideful such as:

❑ I have a stronger desire to do my will than God's will.
❑ I rely on my own strengths and abilities rather than God's.
❑ I too often think my ideas are better than others'.
❑ I want to control how others act rather than develop self-control.
❑ I sometimes consider myself more important than others.
❑ I have a tendency to think I don't need other people.
❑ I find it difficult to admit when I am wrong.
❑ I am more likely to be a people-pleaser than a God-pleaser.
❑ I am overly concerned about getting credit for doing good things.
❑ I often think I am more humble than others.
❑ I often think I am smarter than my parents
❑ I often feel my needs are more important than others' needs.
❑ I consider myself better than others because of my academic, artistic, or athletic abilities and accomplishments.
❑ Other
For each of the above areas that has been true in your life, pray aloud:

Lord, I agree I have been prideful in the area of .... **. Thank You for forgiving me for this pridefulness.**

I choose to humble myself and place all my confidence in You, amen.

Step 6: Bondage vs. Freedom

The next step to freedom deals with the sins that have become habits in your life. Teens who have been caught in the vicious circle of "sin-confess-sin-confess," etc. need to realize that the road to victory is "sin-confess-resist" (see James 4:7).

Habitual sin often requires help from a trusted brother or sister in Christ. James 5:16 says, "Confess your sins to each other and pray for each other so that you may be healed. The prayer of a righteous man is powerful and effective." Seek out a stronger Christian who will lift you up in prayer and hold you accountable in your areas of weakness.

Sometimes, the assurance of 1 John 1:9 is sufficient: "If we confess our sins, he is faithful and just and will forgive us our sins and purify us from all unrighteousness."

Remember, confession is not saying "I'm sorry"; it's openly admitting, "I did it." Whether you need the help of others or just the accountability of God, pray the following prayer aloud:

Dear heavenly Father, You have told us to put on the Lord Jesus Christ and make no provision for the flesh in regard to its lust (see Romans 13:14). **I agree that I have given in to fleshly lusts which wage war against my soul** (see 1 Peter 2:11). **I thank You that in Christ my sins are forgiven, but I have broken Your holy law and given the devil an opportunity to wage war in my body** (see Romans 6:12,13; James 4:1; 1 Peter 5:8). **I come before Your presence now to admit these sins and to seek Your cleansing** (see 1 John 1:9) **that I may be freed from the bondage of sin. I now ask You to reveal to my mind the ways that I have broken Your moral law and grieved the Holy Spirit. In Jesus' precious name I pray, amen.**

There are many habitual sins that can control us. Look through the following list and ask the Holy Spirit to reveal to your mind which of these you need to resolve. Then pray the following prayer for each area.

❏ stealing (shoplifting)
❏ lying
❏ fighting
❏ hatred
❏ jealousy, envy
❏ anger
❏ complaining and criticism
❏ impure thoughts
❏ eagerness for lustful pleasure
❏ perfectionism
❏ cheating
❏ gossiping
❏ other

Lord, I admit that I have committed the sin of..**.**
I thank You for Your forgiveness and cleansing. I turn away from this sin and turn to You, Lord. Strengthen me by Your Holy Spirit to obey You. In Jesus' name, amen.

It is our responsibility to not allow sin to have control over our bodies. We must not use our bodies, or someone else's, as an instrument of unrighteousness (see Romans 6:12,13). If you are struggling with sexual sins you can't stop (such as pornography, masturbation, heavy petting/kissing, oral sex or sexual intercourse) pray as follows:

Lord, I ask You to reveal to my mind every sexual use of my body as an instrument of unrighteousness. In Jesus' precious name I pray, amen.

As the Lord brings to your mind every sexual use of your body, whether it was done to you (i.e., rape, incest, or any sexual molestation) or willingly by you, renounce every occasion:

Lord, I renounce (name the specific use of your body) **with** (name the person involved) **and I ask You to break that sinful bond with him** (or her).

After you have completed the above exercise, commit your body to the Lord by praying aloud from your heart:

Lord, I renounce all these uses of my body as an instrument of unrighteousness, and I admit my willful participation. I now present my body to You as a living sacrifice, holy and acceptable unto You, and I choose to reserve the sexual use of my body for marriage only.

I reject the lie of Satan that my body is not clean or that it is dirty or in any way unacceptable to You as a result of my past sexual experiences. Lord, I thank You that You have totally cleansed and forgiven me, and that You love me just as I am. Therefore, I can accept myself and my body as cleansed in Your eyes. In Jesus' name, amen.

Special Prayers for Specific Needs: Homosexual

Lord, I renounce the lie that You have created me or anyone else to be homosexual, and I agree that You clearly forbid homosexual behavior. I accept myself as a child of God and declare that You created me a man (or a woman). I renounce any bondages of Satan that have perverted my relationships with others. I announce that I am free to relate to the opposite sex in the way that You intended. In Jesus' name, amen.

Abortion

Lord, I confess that I was not a proper guardian and keeper of the life You entrusted to me, and I ask your forgiveness. I choose to accept Your forgiveness by forgiving myself, and I now commit that child to You for Your care for all eternity. In Jesus' name, amen.

Suicidal Tendencies

I renounce the lie that I can find peace and freedom by taking my own life. Satan is a thief, and he comes to steal, kill and destroy. I choose life in Christ, who said He came to give me life and to give it to the full.

Eating Disorders, or Cutting on Yourself

I renounce the lie that my value as a person is dependent upon how I look on the outside. I renounce cutting myself, vomiting, using laxatives or starving myself as a means of cleansing myself of evil or altering my appearance. I announce that only the blood of the Lord Jesus Christ cleanses me from sin. I accept the reality that there may be sin present in me due to the lies I have believed and the wrongful use of my body. But I renounce the lie that I am evil or that any part of my body is evil. My body is the temple of the Holy Spirit and I belong to God. I am totally accepted by God in Christ, just as I am.

Substance Abuse

Lord, I confess that I have misused substances (alcohol, tobacco, food, prescription or street drugs) for the purpose of pleasure, to escape reality or to cope with difficult problems. I confess that I have abused my body and programmed my mind in a harmful way. I have not allowed Your Holy Spirit to guide me. I ask Your forgiveness, and I reject any satanic connection or influence in my life because of my misuse of drugs or food. I cast my cares onto Christ who loves me, and I commit myself to no longer give in to substance abuse, but instead allow the Holy Spirit to lead

me. I ask You, heavenly Father, to fill me with Your Holy Spirit. In Jesus' name, amen.

After you have confessed all known sin, say:

I now confess these sins to You and claim, through the blood of the Lord Jesus Christ, my forgiveness and cleansing. I cancel all ground that evil spirits have gained through my willful involvement in sin. I ask this in the wonderful name of my Lord and Savior Jesus Christ, amen.

Step 7: Curses vs. Blessings

The last step to freedom is to renounce the sins of your ancestors and any curses which may have been placed on you. In giving the Ten Commandments, God said, "You shall not make for yourself an idol in the form of anything in heaven above or on the earth beneath or in the waters below. You shall not bow down to them or worship them; for I, the Lord your God, am a jealous God, punishing the children for the sin of the fathers to the third and fourth generation of those who hate me" (Exodus 20:4-5).

Demonic or familiar spirits can be passed on from one generation to the next, if you don't renounce the sins of your ancestors and claim your new spiritual heritage in Christ. You are not guilty for the sin of any ancestor, but because of their sin, Satan has gained access to your family.

In addition, deceived and evil people may try to curse you, or satanic groups may try to target you.

You have all the authority and protection you need in Christ to stand against such curses. In order to walk free from the sins of your ancestors and any demonic influences, read the following declaration and pray the following prayer aloud. Let the words come from your heart as you remember the authority you have in Christ Jesus.

Declaration:

I here and now reject and disown all the sins of my ancestors. As one who has been delivered from the domain of darkness into the kingdom of God's Son, I cancel out all demonic workings that has been passed down to me from my family. As one who has been crucified and raised with Jesus Christ and who sits with Him in heavenly places, I renounce all satanic assignments that are directed toward me and my ministry. I cancel out every curse that Satan and his workers have put on me. I announce to Satan and all his forces that Christ became a curse for me (see Galatians 3:13) **when He died for my sins on the cross. I reject any and every way in which Satan may claim ownership of me. I belong to the Lord Jesus Christ who purchased me with His own blood. I reject all the blood sacrifices whereby Satan may claim**

ownership of me. **I declare myself to be eternally and completely signed over and committed to the Lord Jesus Christ. By the authority that I have in Jesus Christ, I now command every familiar spirit and every enemy of the Lord Jesus Christ that is influencing me to leave my presence. I commit myself to my heavenly Father, to do His will from this day forward.**

Prayer:

Dear heavenly Father. I come to You as Your child, purchased by the blood of the Lord Jesus Christ. You are the Lord of the universe and the Lord of my life. I submit my body to You as an instrument of righteousness, a living sacrifice, that I may glorify You in my body. I now ask You to fill me with Your Holy Spirit. I commit myself to the renewing of my mind in order to prove that Your will is good, perfect and acceptable for me. All this I do in the name and authority of the Lord Jesus Christ, amen

After Thoughts

Once you have secured your freedom in Christ by going through these seven steps, you may find demonic influences attempting to gain control of your mind again, days or even months later. One person shared that she heard a spirit say to her mind, "I'm back" two days after she had been set free. "No you're not!" she proclaimed aloud. The attack stopped immediately.

You need to realize that one victory does not mean the war has been won. Freedom must be maintained. After completing those steps, one happy girl asked, "Will I always be like this?" I told her that she would stay free as long as she remained in right relationship with God. "Even if you slip and fall," I encouraged, "you know how to get right with God again."

One victim of incredible abuse shared this illustration: "It's like being forced to play a game with an ugly stranger in my own home. I kept losing and wanted to quit, but the ugly stranger wouldn't let me. Finally I called the police (a higher authority), and they came and escorted the stranger out. He knocked on the door trying to regain entry, but this time I recognized his voice and didn't let him in."

What a beautiful illustration of gaining freedom in Christ. We call upon Jesus, the final and most powerful authority, and He escorts the powers of darkness out of our lives.

To maintain your freedom, you must know the truth, stand firm in the Lord and resist the evil one. Seek out a good youth group and Christian fellowship. Commit yourself to regular times of studying the Bible and prayer.

Remember that God loves you and He will never leave you or forsake you.

After Care

Freedom must be maintained. We cannot emphasize that point enough. But you have won a very important battle in an ongoing war. Freedom will remain yours as long as you keep choosing truth and standing firm in the strength of the Lord.

If new memories should surface or if you become aware of "lies" that you have believed or other non-Christian experiences you have had, renounce them and choose the truth. If you realize that there are some other people you need to forgive, Step 3 will remind you of what to do.

Some people have found it helpful to walk through the *Steps to Freedom in Christ* again. As you do, read the instructions carefully.

You should definitely read the books *Stomping Out the Darkness* and *The Bondage Breaker Youth Edition* right away. To maintain your freedom, the following are strongly suggested as well:

1. Get involved in a loving church youth group or Bible study where you can be open and honest with other believers your age.

2. Study your Bible daily. There are many great youth Bibles around for you to use. Begin to get into God's Word and memorize key verses. Remember, it is the *truth that sets you free, and it is the truth that keeps you free!* You may want to say the *Statement of Truth* aloud daily and study the verses.

3. Learn to take every thought captive to the obedience of Christ. Assume responsibility for your thought life. Don't let your mind go passive. Reject all lies, choose to focus on the truth and stand firm in your identity in Christ.

4. Don't drift away! It is very easy to become lazy in your thoughts and slip back into old habit patterns of thinking. Share your struggles openly with a trusted friend who will pray for you.

5. Don't expect others to fight your battles for you. They can't and they won't. Others can encourage you, but they can't think, pray, read the Bible or choose the truth for you.

6. Commit yourself to daily prayer. Prayer is dependence upon God. You can pray these suggested prayers often and with confidence.

Daily Prayer

Dear heavenly Father, I honor You as my Lord. I know that You are always present with me. You are the only all-powerful and only wise God. You are kind and loving in all Your ways. I love You and I thank You that I am united with Christ and spiritually alive in Him. I choose to not love the world, and I crucify the flesh and all its passions.

I thank You for the life that I now have in Christ, and I ask You to fill me and guide me with Your Holy Spirit so that I may live my life free from sin. I declare my dependence upon You, and I take my stand against Satan and all his lying ways. I choose to believe the truth, and I refuse to be discouraged. You are

the God of all hope, and I am confident that You will meet my needs as I seek to live according to Your Word. I express with confidence that I can live a responsible life through Christ who strengthens me.

I now take my stand against Satan and command him and all his evil spirits to depart from me. I put on the whole armor of God. I submit my body as a living sacrifice and renew my mind by the living Word of God in order that I may prove that the will of God is good, acceptable and perfect. I ask these things in the powerful and precious name of my Lord and Savior, Jesus Christ, amen

Bedtime Prayer

Thank You, Lord, that You have brought me into Your family and have blessed me with every spiritual blessing in the heavenly realms in Christ. Thank You, too, for providing this time of renewal through sleep. I accept it as part of Your perfect plan for Your children, and I trust You to guard my mind and my body during sleep. As I have thought about You and Your truth during the day, I choose to let those thoughts continue in my mind while I am asleep. I commit myself to You for Your protection from every attempt of Satan or his demons to attack me during the night. I commit myself to You as my rock, my fortress and my resting place. I pray in the strong name of the Lord Jesus Christ, amen.

Cleansing Home/Apartment/Room

(After removing all articles of false worship from your home/apartment/room including erotic or idolatrous posters and objects, pray this prayer aloud in every room necessary.)

Dear heavenly Father, we know that You are Lord of heaven and earth. In Your power and love, You have given us all things richly to enjoy. Thank You for this place to live. I claim this home for my family as a place of spiritual safety and protection from all the attacks of Satan. As a child of God, seated with Christ in the heavenly realm, I command every evil spirit, claiming ground in the structures and furnishings of this place based on the activities of previous sinful activities, to leave and never return. I renounce all curses and spells against this place. I ask You,

heavenly Father, to post guardian angels around this home (apartment, condo, room, etc.) to guard it from attempts of the enemy to enter and disrupt Your purposes for me. I thank You, Lord, for doing this, and I pray in the name of the Lord Jesus Christ, amen

Living in a Non-Christian Environment
(After removing all articles of false worship from your room, pray aloud in your sleeping area.)

Thank you, heavenly Father, for a place to live and to be renewed by sleep. I ask You to set aside my room (or portion of room) as a place of safety for me. I renounce any worship given to false gods or spirits by other occupants, and I renounce any claim to this room (space) by Satan, based on what people have done here or what I have done in the past.

On the basis of my position as a child of God and a joint heir with Christ who has all the authority in heaven and on earth, I command all evil spirits to leave this place and never to return. I ask You, heavenly Father, to appoint guardian angels to protect me while I live here. I pray this in the name of the Lord Jesus Christ, amen.

Continue to seek your identity and sense of worth through who you are in Christ. Renew your mind with the truth that your acceptance, security and significance is in Christ alone. Meditate on the following truths daily, reading the entire list aloud, morning and evening over the next few weeks.

I Am Accepted:	In Christ
John 1:12	I am a child of God.
John 15:15	I am Jesus' chosen friend.
Romans 5:1	I am holy and acceptable to God (justified).
1 Corinthians 3:16	I am united to the Lord and am one spirit with Him.
1 Corinthians 6:19,20	I have been bought with a price. I belong to God.
1 Corinthians 12:27	I am a part of Christ's Body, part of His family.
Ephesians 1:1	I am a saint, a holy one.
Ephesians 1:5	I have been adopted as God's child.
Colossians 1:14	I have been bought back (redeemed) and forgiven of all my sins.
Colossians 2:10	I am complete in Christ.
I Am Secure:	
Romans 8:1,2	I am free forever from punishment.

Romans 8:28	I am sure all things work together for good.
Romans 8:31	I am free from any condemning charges against me.
Romans 8:35	I cannot be separated from the love of God.
Colossians 3:3	I am hidden with Christ in God.
Philippians 1:6	I am sure that the good work that God has started in me will be finished.
Ephesians 2:19	I am a citizen of heaven with the rest of God's family.
Hebrews 4:16	I can find grace and mercy in times of need.
1 John 5:18	I am born of God and the evil one cannot touch me.

I Am Significant:

Matthew 5:13,14	I am the salt and light for everyone around me.
John 15:1,5	I am part of the true vine, joined to Christ and able to produce lots of fruit.
John 15:16	I am hand-picked by Jesus to bear fruit.
Acts 1:8	I am a Spirit-empowered witness of Christ.
1 Corinthians 3:16; 6:19	I am a temple where the Holy Spirit lives.
2 Corinthians 5:17	I am at peace with God and He has given me the work of making peace between Himself and other people.
2 Corinthians 6:1	I am God's coworker.
Ephesians 2:6	I am seated with Christ in heaven.
Ephesians 2:10	I am God's building project, His handiwork, created to do His work.
Philippians 4:13	I am able to do all things through Christ who gives me strength!

FREEDOM IN CHRIST MINISTRIES

PURPOSE: FREEDOM IN CHRIST MINISTRIES IS AN INTERDENOMINATION-AL, INTERNATIONAL, BIBLE-TEACHING CHURCH MINISTRY WHICH EXISTS TO GLORIFY GOD BY EQUIPPING CHURCHES AND MISSION GROUPS, ENABLING THEM TO FULFILL THEIR MISSION OF ESTABLISHING PEOPLE FREE IN CHRIST.

FREEDOM IN CHRIST MINISTRIES OFFERS A NUMBER OF VALUABLE VIDEO, AUDIO, AND PRINT RESOURCES THAT WILL HELP BOTH THOSE IN NEED AND THOSE WHO COUNSEL. AMONG THE TOPICS COVERED ARE:

Resolving Personal Conflicts
Search for Identity ▪ Walking by Faith ▪ Faith Renewal
Renewing the Mind ▪ Battle for the Mind ▪ Emotions
▪ Relationships ▪ Forgiveness

Resolving Spiritual Conflicts
Position of Believer ▪ Authority ▪ Protection ▪ Vulnerability
Temptation ▪ Accusation ▪ Deception and Discernment
Steps to Freedom

Spiritual Conflicts and Biblical Counseling
Biblical Integration ▪ Theological Basis ▪ Walking by the Spirit
Surviving the Crisis ▪ The Process of Growth ▪ Counseling and Christ
▪ Counseling the Spiritually Afflicted ▪ Ritual Abuse

The Seduction of Our Children
God's Answer ▪ Identity and Self-Worth ▪ Styles of Communication
Discipline ▪ Spiritual Conflicts and Prayer ▪ Steps to Freedom

Resolving Spiritual Conflicts and Cross-Cultural Ministry
Dr. Timothy Warner

Worldview Problems ▪ Warfare Relationships ▪ Christians and Demons
The Missionary Under Attack ▪ Practical Application for
Missionaries ▪ Steps to Freedom in Christ

FOR ADDITIONAL RESOURCES FROM DR. ANDERSON
OR FREEDOM IN CHRIST MINISTRIES WRITE OR CALL US AT:

FREEDOM IN CHRIST MINISTRIES
9051 Executive Park Drive, Suite 503, Knoxville, TN 37923
Phone: (865) 342-4000 Fax: (865) 342-4001
E-mail: info@ficm.org
Web: www.ficm.org